PRAISE FOR *WALK*

"With a bold and honest voice, Jonathon Stalls invites us to walk with him across America. It is an important journey through a landscape of gender, equity, and discovery. In each meeting we learn who we are and who we might become. From sea to sea there are mountains with sticky spines, and deserts filled with people ... and solitude."

—JOHN FRANCIS, PhD, author of *Planetwalker: 22 Years of Walking. 17 Years of Silence.*

"Jonathon and I have been walking and talking together for years. We walk and talk about strategies to create more walkable places, management approaches, dogs, love, relationships—everything.... This book captures the advice that Jonathon has given me over our hundreds of miles together: listen to your inner wisdom, lean into connections, and embrace your failures as a great teaching tool. *WALK* is not just a book. It's designed to take its readers on a meditative journey to enable us to open our eyes to ourselves and each other."

—LYNN RICHARDS, senior VP of policy and implementation at Blue Zones

"Stalls is an important walking activist and his book recounts the adventure of a lifetime."

—ANGIE SCHMITT, author of *Right of Way*

"*WALK* is a powerful invitation that shows us not just the gifts of walking, but what it means to be fully alive.... Stalls reminds us what it means to live with a whole heart, even in the midst of our darkest times, and how walking as an individual and community act—as a fundamental human right— can repair our spirits along with our minds, bodies, and communities."

—ANTONIA MALCHIK, author of *A Walking Life*

"Jonathon Stalls's new book is for all of us who are ready to embark on a journey of practice toward walking and rolling to connect, to build relationships with ourselves and our people, and with intention to build trusting, whole, and full lives.... Whether it is a journey to our mailboxes or the entire length of the continent—this book gives us tools to practice walking and movement to heal, grow, love, nurture, explore, adventure, fight, dance, and become our full human selves. Life at 1–3 mph is how we were intended to experience our world. We must move more this way to feel more and more alive."

—TERESA MARTINEZ, cofounder and executive director of the Continental Divide Trail Coalition

"I've spent the last ten years of my life going on walks with Jonathon Stalls, so I am delighted that in *WALK* more people get to experience his warmth and brilliance too. May you feel what I do after every walk with him: more deeply and uncomplicatedly human."

—NADIA BOLZ-WEBER, three-time *New York Times* best-selling author

"In 2010, on a journey of self healing, Jonathon Stalls set out to walk coast-to-coast across the United States. That defining experience, and years of boot-level community work since, has honed his book into a trail guide to human connectivity—a veritable map of the heart."

—PAUL SALOPEK, Out of Eden Walk

"Jonathon's personal journey is the starting point of a robust community journey, accompanied by heaping helpings of warmth, empathy, compassion, and insight."

—MICHAEL MCGINN, executive director of America Walks and former Seattle Mayor

WALK

WALK

SLOW DOWN, WAKE UP, AND CONNECT AT 1–3 MILES PER HOUR

JONATHON STALLS

North Atlantic Books
Huichin, unceded Ohlone land
aka Berkeley, California

Published by
North Atlantic Books
Huichin, unceded Ohlone land
aka Berkeley, California

Interior art by Jonathon Stalls, Intrinsic Paths
Cover art © zmshv via Getty Images
Cover design by Jasmine Hromjak
Book design by Happenstance Type-O-Rama

Printed in the United States of America

WALK: Slow Down, Wake Up, and Connect at 1–3 Miles per Hour is sponsored and published by North Atlantic Books, an educational nonprofit based in the unceded Ohlone land Huichin (*aka* Berkeley, CA) that collaborates with partners to develop cross-cultural perspectives, nurture holistic views of art, science, the humanities, and healing, and seed personal and global transformation by publishing work on the relationship of body, spirit, and nature.

North Atlantic Books' publications are distributed to the US trade and internationally by Penguin Random House Publisher Services. For further information, visit our website at www.northatlanticbooks.com.

Library of Congress Cataloging-in-Publication Data

Names: Stalls, Jonathon, author.
Title: Walk : slow down, wake up, and connect at 1-3 miles per hour /
    Jonathon Stalls.
Description: Berkeley, Califorinia : North Atlantic Books, [2022] |
    Includes bibliographical references and index. | Summary: "A collection
    of essays on the power of walking to connect with ourselves, each other,
    and nature for new avenues of renewal and change"—Provided by
    publisher.
Identifiers: LCCN 2022000785 (print) | LCCN 2022000786 (ebook) | ISBN
    9781623176952 (trade paperback) | ISBN 9781623176969 (ebook)
Subjects: LCSH: Walking—Psychological aspects. | Walking--Philosophy. |
    Walking--Health aspects.
Classification: LCC RA781.65 .S725 2022 (print) | LCC RA781.65 (ebook) |
    DDC 613.7/176—dc23/eng/20220316
LC record available at https://lccn.loc.gov/2022000785
LC ebook record available at https://lccn.loc.gov/2022000786

1 2 3 4 5 6 7 8 9 KPC 27 26 25 24 23 22

This book includes recycled material and material from well-managed forests. North Atlantic Books is committed to the protection of our environment. We print on recycled paper whenever possible and partner with printers who strive to use environmentally responsible practices.

To the wind, the trees, and millions of
steps for saving my life

CONTENTS

Preface   xi

INTRODUCTION: Walking as Waking Up   1

1   Walking as Human Dignity   19

2   Walking as Humility   39

3   Walking as a Human Right   57

4   Walking as Earth Care   83

5   Walking as Relationship   99

6   Walking as Vulnerability   113

7   Walking as Play   131

8   Walking as Resistance   143

9   Walking as Creative Wonder   159

10 Walking as Presence   171

11 Walking as Rite of Passage   187

12 Walking as Mystery   203

Acknowledgments   215

References   217

Index   219

About the Author   225

PREFACE

You are here ... with all your unique memories, parts, and experiences. As they are.

We are here. In a time where beauty aches to be seen. In a time where our wounds call us closer. In a time where disconnection and separation from our deeper selves, from each other, and our planet grows in devastating ways.

I am humbled and grateful that you have opened this book. I invite you, with courage and wonder, to imagine us, you and I, moving side by side. All that you are next to all that I am. All that I am next to all that you are.

❧

Walking. My most cherished and respected teacher. I have come to know you as a profound and wondrous portal. You have humbly and courageously helped me to nurture my pain, inspire my imagination, release complex suppression, face systemic injustice, honor the cries and gifts of the planet, prioritize mental health, embrace the unknown, and so much more.

We have journeyed for tens of thousands of miles, more than I could ever count, through just about every landscape imaginable. Your pace and posture have helped me to move alongside hundreds of people from a variety of beliefs, abilities, and backgrounds for hours, days, and weeks at a time. You have utterly and completely transformed my one, precious life.

꩜

Dear reader, my education is the brush of wind between you and me while moving alongside each other. My education is the amount of time I have spent by the flowing stream and high-speed arterial roadways. My education is what I feel and experience when having spontaneous exchanges on streets, underpasses, and front porches beyond walls and screens. My education is resting on broken concrete curbs and taking naps under the shade of trees. My education is the one- to three-mile-an-hour manifestation of my own deep truths, shadows, and dreams ... naturally rising like a spring ... slowly surfacing ... so I can tend to them, listen to them, and nurture them the way I believe I was made to.

As I write this book, I am a late-thirtysomething, able-bodied, six-foot-four, white, queer/gay male (he/him/his) in the United States of America who grew up mostly middle-class. My lineage is a nomadic melting pot of people who immigrated to the United States of America from primarily Poland, the Czech Republic (Czechia), Scotland, England, and Ireland. This presents a significant number of privileges, blind spots, and gaps when referencing human movement through a variety of landscapes and neighborhoods. If you are Black, Indigenous, transgender, a person of color, LGBTQIA2S+ (lesbian, gay, bisexual, transgender, queer or questioning, intersex, asexual, two-spirit, and the countless ways people choose to identify), nonbinary, nonconforming, a woman, a person with a disability, a war veteran, an older adult, someone of lower or poverty class, or parents with kids and strollers, then your relationship to walking and rolling, especially wherever or however you want, is more than likely immeasurably different from mine.

If you identify with any of these frames in any sort of way, I honor you and all your uniqueness with all that I have. I also deeply honor the people and lands associated with every tribal nation under the sun. I write and I move with great lament for what has been done

and what continues to be done in the name of colonization, perfection, control, speed, consumerism, greed, and more. I also ache
with all the wonder, beauty, and gifts inside us and around us bursting in the spring and resting in the fall.

With humility, I invite you into a sea of imperfect words. I invite
you to greet them, open your heart around them, question them,
be challenged by them, and more than anything—*move with them.*

INTRODUCTION

WALKING AS WAKING UP

I remember a hawk swirling above us that day. It followed our route for several hours landing on the occasional tree or energy pole. As I continued to look up, I was deeply aware that my relationship to time was dramatically changing. I had time to feel and to be in my senses. I had time to honor the presence of this winged teacher. I had time to notice the way it preened its feathers and gripped the pole with strong, curled claws as it watched us walk by. I smiled, a lot, as it flew. We made eye contact several times throughout the day.

The rain was getting heavier. My head was mostly down to avoid the sting of sideways drops. I was only three days into my cross-country walk. The misty, cloudy, and gloomy wetness of March in Delaware had a romantic effect on me. I felt held by the forested trees and their leaves draped like wet blankets. It was the start of a whole new way of seeing the world, and ultimately, myself. When I watched the flying hawk, I noticed my own desire to soar. When I felt the rain hit my skin, I invited it to wash away fear and unhelpful stories. When I saw the sun peer through the clouds, I could almost touch the warmth of my own inner light.

There we were. Kanoa, my cherished furry friend, and I, moving on the slim shoulder of a winding busy street. This would be my first night without a place to stay. As the setting sun approached, anxiety began to take over. Where would I sleep? My many moments with the hawk, sky, streams, and trees that day helped me to trust that I would land where I needed to land ... and I was still terrified. This day was also my first official state crossing. At my unhurried walking pace, it took me two and a half days to cross into Maryland from Delaware. It felt epic. It was epic. I had never done anything like this. I always encourage people who are interested in a cross-country walking journey to start in Delaware for this reason.

It was still raining and getting darker fast. I was about to make a left turn a mile up the road toward Martinak State Park, which rests along the Choptank River in Maryland. My plan was to call the local ranger to get permission to camp. I also knew that at some point I would need to just put that damn tent down for the night without permission.

The rain started to pick up, and so did our pace. Before too long, I heard a faint voice from the woods behind us. Out of nowhere, from the misty thick forest, a woman came running out waving with one hand and shielding rain with the other.

She greeted us, "Hi! Um, I'm Hailey. Do you mind if I walk with you for a few minutes?"

"Of course! Are you okay? It's pouring out," I said.

She started briskly walking alongside of us. Cars were buzzing by, occasionally splashing us, and I kept remembering Kanoa's face looking back up at me every so often with gratitude and confusion related to the already really long walk. "What is happening? Why is she out here walking with us?" I kept thinking to myself. I was quickly drawn to her lightness and curiosity. She had long brown hair pulled into a ponytail. She had work clothes on with shoes that were not made for walking in the rain. She was, however, plenty fine joining us in the roadside downpour. I loved it.

"I was driving home from work, and I noticed your dog's curly tail. I then saw the 'Kiva Walk Across the USA' sign on your back-pack. I rushed home to check you out online. As soon as I saw your site, I had to know more. I knew if I ran the back way from my house, through the woods, I would catch up to you." We continued walking in the rain. I offered her my rain jacket, and she finally took it. Ten minutes went by, and she stopped.

"Would you like a place to stay?" she said, somewhat quick and light-hearted. "You know, it's pouring. I love animals. I don't want you both out here in the rain. We can have a meal, and I'll just come pick you up when you're done with your route," she finished.

Here we are. Hailey is around five-foot-four and I'm six-foot-four. I am drenched with rain, mud, sweat, and a steamy smell from not showering in two days. Kanoa is drenched, muddy, and looks like a wolf. This woman, with her hands over her eyes, is looking up at me on the side of a state highway asking us if we wanted dinner and a warm, dry place to stay?

Dumbfounded and overjoyed: "Are you sure? Wow! I don't know what to say. I mean, yes! That would be wonderful. But are you sure? This is strange, isn't it? I mean, it shouldn't be. But ... thank you," I fumbled.

There it was. My first trail angel ... someone just showing up, as if out of the sky, with hospitality, heart, life, nourishment, and love. Well before my walk, I reached out to people who had done walks like this. Each of them had used this term "trail angel." It was in my mind, but it landed hard in my heart after meeting Hailey.

The temperature was dropping. I asked Hailey if she would be okay meeting us in an hour at the shopping plaza down the street. She agreed. I put my stealth camping fears away for the night. I knew they were coming for me, and I needed them to, but not tonight.

Hailey came to pick us up. I loved her home. It was colorful and cozy. I walked into her skinny hallway to drop my pack and take off my shoes. She had animal fences, toys, and jungle gyms everywhere. She had seven cats and a rescue dog. We sat on her couch, ate our food, and right away began exchanging meaningful stories. I remember cherishing her laugh. She had such a large and contagious smile with full cheeks and friendly eyes. We covered personal

beliefs, stereotypes, sexual orientation and identity, past relationships, family, fears, pain and hardship, dreams, love of animals,
hope, consumerism, and so much more. My heart was full.

There was no hesitation in sharing just about anything with her.
She is that kind of person, and it was that kind of moment. I remember ruminating before sleeping that night that maybe we all have
the capacity to be these kinds of people if given the right kinds of
moments.

She shared with me that she had never done anything like this,
and since her job was at an animal shelter, she thought that Kanoa
was the sure ticket that we might be okay. "What if I didn't have
Kanoa? What if I was Black or darker-skinned? What if she knew
I had a boyfriend before getting to know me? What if I was wearing a hijab? What if I was a woman? What if I was someone who
was walking in the rain without a home?" I thought to myself. I carried these aches with me throughout my entire journey. They were
important questions for a country and an individual (me) that I felt
like I was getting to know, more fully and more honestly, for the
very first time.

As I ate breakfast reflecting on the night before, I knew that I
would never forget Hailey. I will never forget the way it felt to see
her running out from the woods in the rain with her waving hands
and eyebrows tilted upward. With a wide-open heart and eyes full
of tears, I said farewell to my new friend.

WALKING THE USA

It took 242 days on foot for us to get from the eastern shore of the
Atlantic Ocean in Lewes, Delaware, to Baker Beach in San Francisco.

I will never forget the fear, anxiety, and excitement on that
first day. I had no idea what I was doing, and that was exactly why
I needed to do it. This was my unquestionable rite-of-passage,
coming-of-age experience. It wasn't getting a driver's license. It

wasn't getting my degree. It wasn't rushing to get married and have kids. It wasn't getting a house with an attached garage. It wasn't earning six figures. I am not judging you if you have found beauty, belonging, and joy in these things. They simply didn't work for me. They felt like lies and violations all knotted up in my stomach. The pressure to chase them nearly suffocated me.

I wanted to shed what felt like artificial skin designed by chains and systems I never trusted. I wanted to walk into a new and thicker skin, one that I could boldly claim as my own, for the rest of my days. I wanted to know beyond knowing that "I have what it takes. I have what it takes to feel strong, courageous, honest, and free on the inside so I could be strong, courageous, honest, and free on the outside."

As we reached two weeks, I could not get over how it felt to move for days at a time through neighborhoods, towns, valleys, ranches, farms, rivers, and cities. I depended on my own inner guiding, my body, and the kindness of strangers the whole way through. Having grown up mostly sheltered inside walls and car windshields, my world swiftly expanded, moment by moment, step by step.

I am fully aware that not everyone reading or listening on the other side of these pages will get up and walk across their own country or even their own state. I am also aware of the many barriers that keep so many of us from even walking or rolling for thirty minutes to an hour right outside our own front door. Everything that lives in this book, however, longs for you to consider starting somewhere. Maybe twenty minutes with a friend, maybe meditative loops at a park, or maybe getting lost for a weekend with no destination in mind.

Reaching the family farms of West Virginia, the lakeside laughter in rural Ohio, the soulful songs of Kentucky, the ticks and rivers of Missouri, the grasses and sunsets in Kansas, the courage of the Rocky Mountains, the wild horses of Nevada's high desert, and the everybody-belongs shore of California is with me forever.

Along the way, I raised awareness for an amazing organization called Kiva. They believed in me from the moment they received a big manila envelope containing my wild twenty-five-page, three-thousand-mile idea. Throughout the walk, our Kiva Walk Lending Team generated over half a million dollars in socially responsible loans to entrepreneurs all over the world. The hundreds of people who showed up and crossed my path are my angels, teachers, and heroes. They walked with me, fed me, loved on me, and buried gummy bears, beer, and water in the desert for me.

More than the mileage and the feat of walking across the country, what spoke the loudest for me was the day-by-day acceptance of and reverence to the wisdom of the natural world and the human heart. I felt the trees and rising sun calling out my name every morning as I woke. The songs of strangers spoke of a deep yearning to forever move toward love, trust, nuance, humility, dignity, mystery, healing, and justice. Everything I learned and all of what continues to ache related to my long 242-day walk rumbles in every word of this book.

THE EDGE OF THE ROAD

The following content contains a story and language on suicide attempts and ideation.

Walking in this way saved me. It still saves me. My cross-country walk was a messy, terrifying, and wondrous journey holding the hand of someone who hated and betrayed himself for so many years growing up. When I left the Delaware coast on March 1, 2010, it was primarily to heal, to rise from places consumed by hurt, and to dream.

I nearly attempted suicide at the age of twenty-four. This was in 2006, four years before my long walk. It was in the middle of the night. I wrapped myself up in a blanket and crawled out of the bedroom window. I walked on a rural dirt road with focused determination toward the busier small highway near where I lived. My insides felt like rolling waves of lava. There was an area along the road where you couldn't see the lights of nearby houses in either direction. That's where I stopped. I stood at the edge of the road. I waited for the largest, loudest truck. All I needed to do was take two or three steps, or one large jump. That would be the end. My last night. My last breath.

Deep within, I was lost and locked away. I showed the world the most likeable, conflict-free version I could muster. How I processed the chaos surrounding much of my upbringing, my intuitive rumblings, my artistic heart, and my strong sensitivities was not welcome, or so I thought, in the outside world. I buried it all as far down as I could for my entire childhood, throughout high school, and into my early twenties.

My parents split when I was six. From there, I moved every two years. I was a new student in ten different schools living in a wide variety of urban and rural environments. The idea of "home" was and continues to be complex.

Being the oldest child and extremely sensitive, I learned quickly that I could help diffuse situations by affirming, interpreting, absorbing, and bridging all the pain that was getting flung around me. Fitting in, masking, and reinventing myself to avoid bullying, social anxiety, panic, and conflict was a form of early coping. I love my parents and stepparents deeply. Our relationships have grown and deepened over the years. I cherish and love each of them. I know they cherish and love me. We always had a roof over our heads, nourishing food on the table, and access to an abundance of programs and school activities. These are gifts and privileges that I do not take lightly.

The great gaps I faced, both in and beyond the home, resembled environments nearly absent of emotional transparency, openness about sexuality, healthy spiritual development, healthy conflict, community and neighborhood relationship-building, and connection to the natural world. I also move through the world with deep lineages of alcoholism, depression, and suicide.

A significant ingredient stewing in my adult formation was my attraction to the same sex. At the time it was, at least outwardly, simple. It was a non-option and was never to be made public. On the inside it was radiant, whimsical, confusing, painful, and terrifying.

Ever since seventh grade, I knew. I just knew.

> There he goes again. Whoa, he's beautiful.
> I can't stop looking at him.
> Look quickly. Make sure no one sees you, especially him.
> I'm getting butterflies in my stomach knowing he will be in my
> next class.
> New seat assignments. I hope I get to sit next to him.
> He makes me nervous. Don't stare.
> Does he see me? Does he feel the same way?
> What is happening?
> This is wrong!
> Turn it off, Jonathon.
> No one will accept this.
> Toughen up. Be a real man.
> Finding him beautiful is a sin.
> Draw women. Date women. Dream of being with women.
> God will fix you if you follow the "right" rules and say the
> "right" things.
> Deny your heart.
> Keep the peace.
> Bury your truths until you no longer recognize them.

These voices were heavier and more oppressive than I ever imagined. Add moment-by-moment social and environmental patriarchy, heteronormativity, narrow religious manipulation, and LGBTQIA2S+ violence. All of this piled onto my young heart. A new sharp rock landed on the pile every moment I was bullied for being new or for being sensitive. A new sharp rock landed on the pile every moment pastors preached on love while condemning people to hell. A new sharp rock landed on the pile every time a family member or coach casually spouted "silly boys," "funny boys," "gays," "fags." It all piled up in galaxies of pain.

Oh, the storm of emotions that would rise as I stood on the edge of the road waiting for the right truck. *"I don't have what it takes. I am too sensitive, emotional, artsy, angry, and queer. Belonging is not for me. My existence is weak and blank. All my paths end in despair.*

The destruction inside got louder and louder. It held my toes on the edge of the pavement, giving me blazing permission to jump. In trying to draw up the courage to jump, I would speak awful things out loud and into my stomach where it all seemed to swirl. *"I'm inauthentic trash. I am weak. I am too sensitive for this world. Fuck you, Jonathon, for being spineless and inauthentic. You are on the edge of this road because you have no ground to stand on."*

I stood there wiping my eyes, punching my stomach, and shivering. I would unquestionably hurt people if I decided to love who I was. I and everyone would be better off if I ended it now.

> The
> wind
> in
> the
> trees.

I will never forget it. The way the branches and leaves roared above me. It was 2 a.m. and there was a solid, quiet break in traffic. I gazed at the night sky, found myself in the stars, and stared at the tree-branch silhouettes as they danced with the moonlight. Haunting and liberating. I still see them to this day. The wind and the bending, stretching, and reaching branches cleverly guided me to slowly lift my foot from the edge and pace along the road. I started to walk, skirting the edges of gravel and grass. Even though I had stepped off, I was far from ready to abandon my plan.

I kept looking up at the trees. I closed my eyes to feel the wind. I started moving faster, and I noticed that I naturally started moving away from the road. The stars were getting brighter. The moonlight felt warm.

I survived.

We—the trees and I—broke a big chain that day. It was not an easy road after that, but there was no jumping in front of traffic. There was no falling into the abyss of lies. My relationship to trees, sky, stars, and wind has never been the same.

WAKING UP TO MY ARTISTIC, QUEER, AND SENSITIVE HEART

As I have grown closer and closer to a full-bodied relationship to walking as a practice, as an intrinsic tool, as a way of being in the world, I have simultaneously grown closer and closer to my colorful, complex, and worthy inner journey. I have learned that the natural world around me, which includes other human beings like you, is really one giant mirror into my deepest aches, wounds, and dreams. Moving in an unhurried way for hours or days or weeks at a time has allowed me to tend to and nurture these truths in ways I would have never thought possible. As I took more time to move with the details of a twisted branch reaching for the sun, the raw life experiences living in strangers, and the way flowing water rests and rushes along, the more I moved with my own reaching, my own rawness, and my own resting and rushing.

While it may never fully go away, I can shout with joy and self-love to no longer weave my identity, worthiness, and sense of belonging to exclusive, capitalistic, and conditional systems and "Gods." I have come to deeply believe that my color, my capacity to love, my artistic expression, my LGBTQIA2S+/gay identity, and my rumbling intuition belong. As they are. As it is. As I am. I want to live a life that is awake to my deep truths, the deep truths in you, the deep truths in the natural world, and all the mystery, questions, and imperfections in between it all. My coming-out journey wasn't just accepting my cosmic queer existence, but it was also accepting my sensitive heart, my love for creative expression, and my dreams around a more honest, genuine, simple, peaceful, just, nonbinary, and less extractive way in this life.

Walking helps me mold, tend, and shape these truths in ways that never feel forced or transactional. Walking also teaches me about flow. It helps me invite the raw and complex rainbow blazing between my lived experience and yours. Walking unquestionably, and almost immediately, brings me into direct relationship with human and planet landscapes that are inherently too wondrous to be defined, too expansive to be fully grasped, and in the end, full of stars.

A PROBLEMATIC DEEP SLEEP

I often swirl in thought, art-making, and movement around the very environments that didn't nourish or allow me and so many others to feel seen, affirmed, loved, and connected. We face weary and delicate times. Screens and ads attempt everything imaginable to hijack our capacity to hear, follow our hearts, and trust what aches in our stomachs. Screens and ads fight to keep us feeling worthless and purposeless without their many things, fads, accessories, toys, and dramas. The fear, anger, and shame we carry cries out for more nurturing people and systems. Our capacity to be with nuance and compassion is literally giving way beneath us.

Strings of money feed on our personal and collective ability to numb, avoid, and project the pain we carry. Strings of money block rightful relationship to the natural world. Strings of money want you and me to get "in line" and cast out those who challenge us. Strings of money celebrate and profit on you and me bypassing any and all attempts to slow down, heal, and repair.

We are in a problematic deep sleep.

As I walk, often eight to fifteen miles a day, I absorb endless amounts of beauty, wonder, pain, and devastation. Moving in this way unquestionably impacts my attentiveness and care for how I show up, how I listen, and how I evolve. More than anything, it *wakes me up.* It wakes me up to my intuition. It wakes me up to tenderness and compassion. It wakes me up to the language of land and streams. It wakes me up to the spaces between artificial lines and binaries. It wakes me up to the dehumanizing effects of emails and tweets. It wakes me up to my own fumbling, fragility, and humility.

Walking and rolling with a spirit of listening, opening, and healing is vastly different than one of conquering, separating, and extracting. Waking up demands for us to throw off the covers that block us from greater depths of love, connection, healing, justice, and belonging. Waking up will rattle our bones. Waking up will cost us. Waking up will also nurture, connect, and heal us.

BIRTHING WALK2CONNECT

Stay awake. Keep connecting. Keep moving. These words, like sacred agreements, radiated loud in my heart while plunging into the ocean at the end of my cross-country walk. They spoke directly to how I wanted to design my life in the days ahead while also creating invitation for others along the way. They felt like the bridge that invited people from isolation and separation to healing and belonging. Much like leaving the Delaware coast in early 2010, I knew that I would have to jump, yet again, into the unknown. I sourced my graphic art education and created a logo and an official group on Meetup. I called it Walk2Connect. My first few scheduled walks were twenty-five-mile loops in a day. Nobody showed up. I was humbled but not surprised. I reduced it to eighteen miles, and three people joined. We had a magical time. That was all the confirmation I needed to keep going, to keep trying. Walk2Connect started as an artistic, grassroots experiment, and that is exactly how I would describe it still today.

As I started to add more walks on the calendar, more people wanted to join. Soon, they wanted walking events closer to their home and for a less ambitious amount of time. With the help of amazing cocreators, we started training leaders, and off they went. The website went up in 2012 and the tag #lifeat3mph was born in 2013. Fast-forward to 2016, and what was a humble social business called Walk2Connect LLC became the first worker-owned walking cooperative of its kind. Today, Walk2Connect continues to be a grassroots community with a beautiful network of walking and rolling leaders and friends across the globe who share a vision to connect and move the way we're made to. Our wondrous network has and continues to help inspire hundreds of unique connection-focused walks (and rolls) throughout the year. Our invitations span themes (or no themes) related to public health, social connection, land conservation, pedestrian safety education, bilingual and cross-cultural connecting, spiritual and emotional well-being, youth leadership, and more.

My work with Walk2Connect has continued to add thousands upon thousands of miles alongside hundreds of people to my always blossoming walking journey. As a multidisciplinary "walking artist," the canvas in front of us—you and me—for how we engage, prioritize, and live into this not-so-ordinary intrinsic modality is eagerly waiting for us. Our planet is longing to be seen and nurtured; people are longing to be seen and nurtured; and our own spirits and inner truths are longing to be seen and nurtured. We must keep moving.

CENTERING PEDESTRIAN DIGNITY

The inequities and injustices facing all who walk or use a wheelchair as their primary form of transportation shake me to my core. The lack of ease, safety, comfort, and access for all who would choose to walk or roll for health, connection, and fresh air shakes me to my core. The gaps are wide and devastating between those who drive, those who influence transportation systems, and the raw lived experience of people walking or rolling. Over the years, I have been experimenting and curating a creative storytelling campaign called Pedestrian Dignity. As I write this book, I have had worlds of mostly young people engaging and affirming this ache in waves.

Take a moment to think about pedestrians or people using wheelchairs in most North American non-urban-core settings. They stand out, often in a sea of concrete. They are often perceived as threatening, suspicious, or disruptive by drivers, homeowners, property owners, and police. Whether you are in a rural town or village, a small or medium-size city, or a suburb, it is only becoming more prevalent and practical that the only transportation option is a single-occupant vehicle. This is, of course, impossible for those who cannot drive. It is beyond dangerous for those who fear driving or are advised not to drive. It is discouraging and often beyond comprehension for those who entertain the idea of choosing not to drive.

This is not car-shaming. I am not making the automobile itself the enemy. I personally enjoy occasional trips by car. I relish getting out, away, or up and above within a matter of minutes. I personally depend on systems supporting bus transportation. I am grateful for what the automobile can do to take young kids, older adults, or people with various disabilities to places they may never get to see. I am grateful for the automobile in giving many people the freedom to participate and belong in a variety of spaces. I am deeply grateful for what benefits us by way of trucking and shipping. There are many complex gifts to this adventurous mode of transportation.

I also feel it is deeply important to name the role automobiles play in helping many people feel publicly and socially safe. With many of our origins and destinations sprawled out for miles between one another, there are often weary amounts of isolation and exposure. If we are not actively working to repair the harms of systemic racism, classism, homophobia, gender discrimination, catcalling, and all forms of oppressive human othering, walking or rolling in public becomes dangerous and life-threatening. This is on top of an already devastating transportation environment. We cannot start to create spaces of personal, social, and public trust with non-automobile transportation if our environments remain inaccessible and hostile to walking, using a wheelchair, and taking the bus.

As developers, decision-makers, and the greater public continue designing, approving, and building common places—home, work, school, social centers, and health clinics—that are dependent on the automobile and hostile to all other forms of transportation, we face devastating gaps around how our bodies, minds, emotions, social fabric, and spirits were made to move, connect, and evolve. Everything inside me believes that the demands of today's automobile lobby is one of the most significant contributors keeping us from healing political and social divides, providing equitable public safety and health, and radically tending to the needs of the biosphere. In each and every walk or roll you take, I am inviting you to face, challenge, and repair harmful transportation systems with me while radically centering the needs of today's pedestrian.

INTRINSIC MOVEMENT AND THE PORES OF YOUR SKIN

Throughout the entirety of this book, the term *walking* is inclusive to moving at an unhurried pace on a wheelchair, powered scooter, or walker. It is also generally inclusive to hiking since hiking is simply a term for walking in natural environments or at a vigorous pace. I often hear people say, "I am a hiker, not a walker," or "I am a biker, not a walker." This differentiation, mostly only in the United States, always communicates to me that a fast-paced consumer culture has driven itself so deep into one's psyche that it has created a need to separate exercise or a sport from something so fundamentally human.

While I cherish what words can stir, I want the true wisdom to move through *the pores of your skin.* I want you to feel so full of

desire, curiosity, agency, body-vibration, trembling, and readiness
that you feel energized to close these pages mid-sentence and dive
immediately into practice. There are no rules, only suggestions,
tips, nudges, and invitation.

YOUR UNIQUE PATH

For each chapter, I have shared personal stories, stories written by
people I love, personal reflections, some of my pen-and-ink art-
work, and a host of practices. The practices I have included might
serve as relationship tools, personal activities, therapeutic nourishment, team building, communal blessings, and experiential class-
rooms. There are some incredible books out there with oceans of
facts, data, research papers, articles, and science that back up every
ache branching out of these pages. I have referenced several of
them throughout the book. Seek them.

For some of you, trying on these invitations will allow for an
unending horizon of new experiences that will nourish, humble, and
teach you. For others, it might be revisiting, reframing, or refining
how you already connect and hold space while walking or rolling.
Many of these invitations will fit, and perhaps many will not. Honor
your own stories, twists, turns, challenges, and reflections. Plan on
the mystery of it all to bless and perhaps disappoint in plenty.

While there are threads of intention woven into how each
chapter and theme is presented, there is no formal order. Honor
how you are showing up, and feel encouraged to skip themes and
jump around. If one theme or practice calls to you, stick with it. You
might move with that same theme or practice for weeks or months
at a time. Try one practice in a host of different environments. Try
a handful of practices in the same environment. You might invite
themes that feel more comfortable or accessible at first and then
move into one that might make you more uncomfortable a little
further on.

Try, with everything you have, to honor body-based knowledge. Release expectations and all temptations to overthink. Be open and curious. Absorb the invitations and move into practice as soon as you can. Create your own paths, art, poetry, and stories as you move. Feel the ground, listen for the breeze, trace the birds, follow the trees, and look to the sky.

AN IMPERFECT WAY

Here we are. A place where my imperfect words and life experiences meet your precious life and unique story. Trust that I continue to drum up these aches with you. There is no arriving. It seems, at least for me, to be only uncovering, listening, releasing, and emerging. We are weaving a tapestry, dancing in spirals, and often returning to familiar places with no end in sight. Let us lean into believing the best in each other throughout this experience. You are worthy because you breathe. You are worthy because you exist.

I do hope some of my messy unaffiliated truths invite you, as you really are, into a wondrous field of authenticity, awakening, deep healing, unquestionable justice, curiosity, and human becoming. Moving in this way has allowed me, more times than not, to radically love who I am in this life. Waking up to what is actually going on inside of us and around us is no easy task. And, wise unhurried movement, help us try.

the dignity in me honors the dignity in you
the courage in me honors the courage in you
the truths in me honor the truths in you
the rage in me honors the rage in you
the pain in me honors the pain in you

the love in me
honors
the love in you

1

WALKING AS HUMAN DIGNITY

SHOULDER TO SHOULDER

Our arms are swinging, and the landscape is slowly moving along-side of us. The Colorado air wraps itself around our cheeks, our breath, and our bodies. The sky is big and open. It feels good to be outside, away from the walls.

Our walking group finds itself every Thursday around 10:30 a.m. in the sprawling and concrete-covered corners of southeast Denver. International markets, large corporate office buildings, strip malls, spacious parking lots, service centers, and busy arterial streets cover the landscape.

The women on this weekly walk are from Iraq. They are refu-gees, and they came to the United States just after the U.S.-Iraq war and are mostly all over the age of sixty-five.

We walk, all nine of us, side by side. Some of us right next to each other, some holding hands, and others behind or in front. Humble glances and friendly smiles are exchanged. Some of the women bring their previous conversations into a moving dialogue, and some hardly talk at all, if ever. We seem to subconsciously agree that there's enough in the outside world keeping our attention and connection without words.

Most of the women are Muslim and wear colorful or all-black hijabs. A few of them are Christians with uncovered strawberry-blond hair. I love sharing breakfast together before going on the walks. We all sit around a table, across all our ideas and differences. Their culture, their language, their foods, and their traditions of home bring them together beyond their conflicting beliefs. Most of these families fought on the side of the United States during the U.S.-Iraq war. Most of them have lost immediate loved ones in the war: sons, husbands, brothers, sisters, and cousins—gone. Tears well up in their eyes, and in mine, every time it comes up on our walks. They are grateful to the United States for their role in the war; however, many of them miss the culture and roots of their homeland. They share with me that they are angry and sad for the state of their home country, and with gratitude are doing whatever they can to make things work here in the United States. I will never forget two of the women coming up to me in early 2017 when our country had a ban on Iraqi refugees. They asked, "We are looking at places to go. We don't feel safe here in Colorado. We feel there are better states to live in. What do you think? Would Oregon be better for us? Please tell us. We'll move. Do you know people in Oregon?"

I had no answers for them.

Their words filled me with grief. It felt like fire rising up in my chest. The unnecessary mistrust, disconnection, and devastation when a country and culture feel threatened by those they don't understand. I so badly wished there were more people in our city living in relationship with these incredible women and their beautiful families to affirm that they are welcome here, right where they are, as they are.

We're still walking. Without words we are still listening and connecting to one another. Most of the time I carry a wide smile but am silent. I can't speak Arabic, and you can only say, "How are you? What is new?" so many times when the answer is met with a humble grin and a squint. We end up connecting, eagerly, around everything else. I pick up sticks, point out plants, encourage stretching motions, offer up dance shuffles, and more. In some ways, it is refreshing to move beyond spoken forms of communication. We laugh, and we move. Nature, along with one another's company, feels good, and is always enough.

After having guided so many group walking experiences, I have utmost trust for what takes place when the body starts to move in this way. The fluids, the cells, the neurons, and so much more are given permission to lead and to live.

I always show up with a wooden walking stick. The women always ask me why I have it. "You are young," they say. "Why do you have this? To protect us from the dogs?" They laugh and continue. They want to touch it and try it. They always find it to be an entertaining part of our journey together. In fact, as my hair grows longer, past my shoulders, I'm now getting welcomed as "Thor" and "Jesus" by the women and the men every time I walk into the adult day-care center. I feel blessed, in that strange way, to be a frequent target for a good late-morning joke.

The streets we walk are full of parking lots, wide roads, and tiny or nonexistent sidewalks pushing us into traffic. It's no mystery why so many people give in to being sedentary and inside.

We are all waiting and huddling at the fragile pedestrian island facing a high-traffic intersection awaiting our great crossing to the Cherry Creek. The cars rush past us six lanes deep in all directions. I often see the women lock elbows and stand close together as one body.

We cross the street. I find myself doing a quick blessing after we all make it safely. It's frightening, but the rewards are worth it. We continue walking. The glow of the sun off the grasses is calming, no matter the season. Ducks and geese float along the creek, and the sound of the rushing water begins to compete with that of the traffic.

I'll never forget one of our first group walks all the way down to the water.

We were taking a break to enjoy the sun. As we rested, one of the women quietly tiptoed down to the cold creek. She held a small paper cup with one hand and lifted her long skirt with the other. She kneeled and filled her small cup with the cold creek water. Having no care for her friend's dress and mall shoes, she came up from behind and began to pour water onto her head. "Ah-hee-oow!" Everyone's attention quickly focused on the woman who was now wet with creek water. I was waiting for my first group fight or a good long laugh. We waited. She busted out laughing. Thank everything. All of the women roared, and if it wasn't for some of her discomfort getting down the rocks, she would have surely returned the favor to her bold peer. We laughed the whole way back. The playfulness was magic.

As the walks come to a close, words of gratitude in English and in Arabic move between us. The women smile and are grateful to rest. I've been told by the people we work with that this is one of the most valuable programs they have ever had.

Walks like these profoundly change me from the inside out. It's a practice of giving oneself to what can be learned or gained through experience and not just ideas of the mind. Once this embodiment takes shape and begins to live within you, the mind often has no choice but to let go and to adapt. You move with, cry with, and laugh with the story and the song of who you walk with.

There is no turning back to what were only ideas.

Because of this walk, I am forever connected to older women, to refugees from Iraq, to the U.S.-Iraq war, to the many expressions living within Muslim life and so much more, in a way that I would have never imagined. No article or book or political lean would have educated me in this way.

I'm no expert, but I am sure, especially after all our walks, that the questions, the mysteries, the relationships, and the spaces between what we deem is right and what we deem is wrong are more important than ever.

INTEGRATION PRACTICE: RE-SPECT AND THE SECOND GAZE

As you move, take several minutes to be with the root meaning of the word, respect. To re-spect, to look again. When you are out moving and you see someone approaching, sitting on a bench, leaning against a front porch, or waiting in their car at the traffic light, honor their dignity by noticing and going beyond your first reaction. Honor this same invitation with plants, trees, and animals. Move into a practice of intentionally seeing for a second time and drawing out more curiosity, presence, and connection.

MOVING WITH

When you and I move alongside one another, we are actively expanding our capacity to coexist. We invite and encourage shared experience and dialogue. It anchors us into a more primal way of being. How often are we examining and evolving around *how* we learn, lean in, and connect with the unique life experience of another? An unhurried pace that is patient, open, undefended, and humble is a force, especially in this time. Dr. John Francis, one of my personal heroes and author of *Planetwalker,* who walked for seventeen years in silence, shares,

> Listen actively to learn. Be prepared to hear something new without judgment and listen to what you have heard before from the place where you are now. Learning may come from a new understanding of what you already seem to know (Francis 2009, 83).

The consumption machine wants us to avoid what is raw and frag-ile related to our personal and shared existence. It demands for us to numb pain and ignore all signals to live a more honest and present life. It works day and night to have us define our lives and relationships by what we consume (or produce), how much we consume (or produce), and how often we consume (or produce). Moving in a way where one's posture on the Earth is tender and attentive is healing and radical in it of itself. When you move this way, eye contact, common struggle, and time begin to thread chords of trust and connection. These embodi-ments allow for any number of invitations to more organically and authentically know, listen, and learn from other people and our deeper selves, right where they are, right where we are.

More elbow-to-elbow, hip-to-hip, heart-to-heart, and wheels-to-feet human listening, opening, and connecting is such a tangi-ble thing each of us can do to weave connection in this time. As we move, the radical diversity of the planet moves with us, allowing us to be curious, open, and loving alongside the radical diversity in each other. Our journey to each other drastically needs more prac-tices, tools, and spacious environments to inspire more flowing, nuanced, and dignified connection.

INTEGRATION PRACTICE:
SAFE IN ONESELF

Take a moment to read this invitation from Thich Nhat Hanh:

Walk and touch peace every moment

Walk and touch happiness every moment

Kiss the Earth with your feet

The Earth will be safe,

when we feel safe in ourselves (Hanh 2001, 194).

These words, especially the last two lines, ring so loud for me. They move with me wherever I go. Pause for a moment. Close your eyes. Connect with your breath. Invite compassion. After a moment, return to the quote and slowly read it again. If you feel captivated by these words, consider writing them down and taking them with you (yes, now!) as you walk or roll. As you begin your movement, read them again, and perhaps again, with openness and courage, inviting them further into your heart and body. Try replacing "we" with "I" and "ourselves" with "myself." Notice how this reaches into your complex, imperfect, and wondrous life journey. Keep moving and listening for what this invitation stirs in you. You don't need to solve anything. Be with it. Feel each of these words like wind swirling around your swinging arms. I also invite you to try replacing "The Earth" with the name of a person you might invite on a walk. Maybe this is someone who is different than you or someone you have conflict with. Close your movement with gratitude and deep breaths.

MADE FOR MOVEMENT

Human dignity breathes with us. It lives in us. It moves with us. It is us. If we can recognize our own humanity and the needs of our unique body and heart, then the opportunities to better recognize the humanity of another and their unique needs are more awake within us. I want you to imagine the flow of your cells moving through your heart and veins. I want you to picture your lungs expanding as oxygen moves in and out. I invite you to touch the scabs, wrinkles, and stories on your skin. Peer into the small follicles of hair that grow from your skin. Connect to your bones, eyes, ears, and throat.

Pause for a moment to honor the gift of being alive. As you pause, honor just how incredible it is that so many of your unique parts are already *in motion*. We are never, actually, still. Our systems circulate, and our planet constantly rotates while circling the sun. We are made for movement.

Many doctors and researchers show us what happens to the brain, spine, heart, tendons, muscles, and overall circulation of the body after just twenty to thirty minutes of walking. One of these authors, Shane O'Mara, a brain researcher and neuroscientist, shares with us in his book *In Praise of Walking,*

> We all know that it is good for our heart. But walking is also beneficial for the rest of our body. Walking helps protect and repair organs that have been subject to stresses and strains. It is good for the gut, assisting the passage of food through the intestines. Regular walking also acts as a brake on the aging of our brains, and can, in an important sense, reverse it.... Reliable, regular, aerobic exercise can actually produce new cells in the hippocampus, the part of the brain that supports learning and memory. Regular exercise also stimulates the production of an important molecule that assists in brain plasticity.... The phrase "movement is medicine" is correct: no drug has all of these positive effects (O'Mara 2019, 11).

In addition to what Shane names here, consider joint health, healthy circulation, posture, muscle and tendon strengthening, reduction of back pain, and so much more. There are also numerous and sorely underrepresented mental and emotional health benefits beyond just brain development and capacity. Have you heard of eye movement and desensitization reprocessing (EMDR) treatment? While there is much still to learn and understand about the theory of EMDR, the very act of walking led to its birth. Francine Shapiro created EMDR in 1987 when she was walking in a park. She experienced reduced negativity in thoughts and emotions related to troubling memories while she moved and scanned (eyes moving left to right, right to left) her environment. That experience inspired her to focus more energy on the benefits of bilateral stimulation as it relates to healing trauma and emotional well-being (EMDR Institute, 2020).

The benefits to our bodies are endless and wondrous. Our physiological thriving is woven deeply into our movement. We all deserve to move the way we are made to. We all deserve to feel and honor our dignity because we exist.

GIVE ME THE FREEDOM TO WALK

Pam Jiner is a dear friend of mine and someone I consider a profound teacher in my midst. We have coguided and cocreated many walking and rolling events, pedestrian equity actions, and more alongside her Montbello Walks initiative. She was the 2017 Organizer of the Year with the one-of-a-kind organization GirlTrek. Her leadership is for the record books.

Walking as a Black woman is dangerous. It is a threat to my safety. Why are cars and trucks full of white people swooping past me while dumping their coffee, honking their horn, and calling me names? Why are they laughing at me, pointing at me, and throwing their cans out the window toward me? Why, when I walk by white people, do they avoid looking at me and not say anything?

Why don't you see me?

It's not okay. I don't treat white people the way white people treat Black people. My community experiences things like this all the time. Be with this. We live this every day trying to walk on public streets. These streets belong to us too.

Let my people walk.

Give me the freedom to walk.

Imagine a world where we put an end to racism. How much better would it be for everyone? We would all find more natural connections on the streets. We would see and be with each other on the way to work. We would more naturally honor one another's humanity because we are all out here moving together. Taking care of one another would be an act of pride, of dignity. We would be treated with respect as a collective of walkers. We hate what was done to us. We hate what is still being done to us. We are rightfully triggered by racism. I do not believe that people of color are out there to attack and be better than white people.

We just want to live.

It is not all bad. This kind of work makes us all better. There is so much good in the world. I am thankful for white allies. To be clear, not saviors on white horses.

People who are genuinely concerned and genuinely offended.

People who show up with you and speak truth to power.

People who get into the feeling of it all.

People who honor this work every day.

I walk and move with this fear every time I am out. I walk to not feel defeated and to stay healthy, awake, and connected. I take my children with me so they don't feel defeated. It can all be so stressful. It is an awkward balancing act, especially when we also have to navigate and survive streets not designed for pedestrians.

Let my people walk.

Give me the freedom to walk.

Pam's story and the many experiences offered by my Black, Indigenous, people of color, and LGBTQIA2S+ peers related to walking or rolling in the public realm move with me everywhere I go. If we are to take dignity seriously, we must humbly and courageously do everything we can to face, repair, and heal anything that puts one's safety, freedom, and health on the line.

WHITE SUPREMACY, DEVASTATING SEPARATION, AND UNCONDITIONAL LOVE

What, systemically, makes moving the way we are made to easier for some and harder for others? Are we truly willing to open our hearts toward and wake up to the actual breath-by-breath invitation of human dignity? Over the years, the canyons in my stomach have only gotten louder around the harm of unchecked and unfaced systems that slice up and separate people by race, class, sexual orientation, ability, and so on. I feel that if we are to seek genuine, open, and spacious movement with a variety of people who are different than we are, we must get messy and honest about the root of all this pain.

White supremacy.

For me, it resembles a systemic choke hold that clings to and pushes white, wealthy, straight, Christian, colonized, and cis-male (and their families) ideas, agendas, and experiences over the wisdom and lived reality of everyone else. Slowly and compassionately read that again. You might try placing your hand on your heart, while breathing deeply as you reread.

If you identify as white, this isn't a personal attack. I identify as white, and I swim in the waters of white supremacy. White supremacy hurts all of us. This same choke hold also shuts out and warps the deeper truths, wounds, colors, and emotions aching in all of us. While white-identifying folks systemically benefit from moving through the world in white skin, white supremacy lives and works in all races, political parties, religions, and classes. We all swim in it because the very water so many of us have grown up in was formed by it and is still very much maintained by it.

This doesn't mean we are evil people.

This doesn't mean that if you are white, you are an evil person.

This is an invitation to let go, open our hearts, and face hard inner and outer truths.

My harmony-seeking spirit yearns for times and spaces that free us from the ills of devastating separation. I find that unhurried, side-by-side movement gives us miracle-like glimpses into this healing reality. It is why "Walking as Human Dignity" is the first chapter in this book. Until housing, health care, public transit, water treatment, food production, education, generational wealth, religion, and land ownership systems honor and reflect the beloved dignity of all who were and continue to be systemically separated by race, class, sexual orientation, background, ability, and age, we must find creative ways to face, repair, and heal from the harm.

Wounded lineages and practices leave all of us with voids of unfaced, unhealed grief. If we are not tenderly and courageously "walking or rolling this out" with our deeper selves and each other, than we continue (a) feeding various forms of empire ("us against them") or (b) burying it for generations to come. This buried pain eventually projects itself onto those we love, our wondrous planet, and our capacity for radical compassion. How could it not? No wonder we see it erupting in anger (physical and emotional violence), shame (self-hatred and emotional manipulation), and fear (extraction and scarcity), leaving so many of us spiraling in illness, disconnection, and death.

What is unconditional love asking of us?

I invite you back to slowly moving alongside those who are different than you. Your bodies are humbly moving. The sky opens. The wind swirls in the branches. Unhurried, side-by-side movement can act as a courageous balm, nurturing our complex wounds. While solving things may fumble out after months of movement, it is more about tending to canyons and wounds. I have and continue to move with people from all sides of every category under the sun. I remain imperfectly open, brave, fierce, loving, grounded, and curious. These experiences—hundreds of them—have radically opened my heart related to the profound dignity in all of creation while also making systemic justice, collective healing, and humble repair unquestionable.

DEDICATED PRACTICE

Take some time to move with the practice below. Do you know the Indigenous tribal lands you are walking or rolling on? Learn from and honor them as you move. Listen to your body. Honor your needs. Honor the lived reality of all who walk or use a wheelchair as their primary form around you. Honor what will work for you, especially depending on your ability, community, and context. No rules. Only invitation.

Walking as Connection

adrienne maree brown (2017) writes: "Move at the speed of trust. Focus on critical connections more than critical mass—build the resilience by building the relationships."

Creating moving environments where a group of people can let down some of their guard, open up with others, notice the world around them, and check in with their deeper selves inspires me to no end. Throughout my time at Walk2Connect and beyond, I have hosted uncountable walking experiences rooted in connection and trust. We all benefit from spaces that help us feel seen. We all benefit from practices that push us to fumble with words, questions, and responses to get to know people who are different than we are. We all benefit from creative approaches that move us away from walls, screens, positions, and affiliations and into one another's physical, energetic vibration.

There are endless arrangements for how to shape a practice like this. I have listed some examples below and have chosen to focus on the formation of a group. Movement with a group, when nurtured and cared for, can be an incredible pathway to human dignity. I have seen thousands of people experience profound healing, connection, and understanding across a wide variety of lines and differences when moving this way.

Planning: Protect some time to discern the kind of intention you (or you and a cohost, or you and a team) would like to have for your group experience. This could involve thinking on who, specifically, you want to invite or the kind of audiences you are seeking. It could involve a theme or topic that helps you shape dialogue and helps people self-select into your group. It could involve the kind of route you create and story you want it to tell as your group moves through it. It could involve the style of walk you want to host related to prompts, activities, dress, practices, pace, and more. It could also be a little bit of everything. A few examples:

Audience:

- Organize people who live in a specific neighborhood or apartment complex: weekly or monthly invitations, get-to-know or connection experiences, moving scavenger hunts, walk or roll with local representatives.

- Curate experiences where you intentionally invite certain people: new families with young babies, cross-religious or cross-political connection experiences, LGBTQIAS2+ or people of color connection experiences, monolingual Spanish-speaking mothers, people who are trained as master gardeners, people over or under a certain age, couples, mental health walks for nurses and medical workers, pet owners.

Theme:

- Invite someone to teach, present, or guide programming alongside your walking and rolling group: an herbalist on local plants, a forest ranger in a nearby state park, water conservation education, pedestrian safety with an urban planner, contemplative or meditative movement, improv comedy, a musical teacher with songbooks for participants to sing while on the move, medicine and wellness with doctors and healers, a spoken word poet.

- Create prompts around a certain topic and have those prompts guide dialogue and discussion with your walking or rolling group: weekly walks or rolls focused on philosophy, dreams, mental health, or equity, monthly invitations with annual preset topics, experiences that move through signs or stages such as twelve-step, Enneagram, astrological signs, new or full moons.

Route:

- Hyperlocal loops that connect within a specific neighborhood; longer-distance experiences that bridge connection between neighborhoods, historic districts, or landmarks; visiting public art sites; following rivers or creeks; connecting parks and open space; destination-focused, such as a sacred site, a public event, city hall.

Style:

- Fitness and health-focused (stretches, workouts, calories); meditative (silence, deep breathing, additional practices mixed in); artistic expression or activity (walk and sketch, sidewalk chalk breaks, song or performance); dress (costume, reenactment); social (connection, sharing stories).

Preparation and Invitation: Before inviting people to join, protect time to scout your route. This is such an important stage in creating an experience that builds trust. It will allow you to feel comfortable with your route so you can focus on supporting connection and safety among your group. Your route won't have everything, but everyone will benefit from making it as inclusive, safe, and comfortable as possible. You will also benefit from communicating what your route does or doesn't have for people to self-select in or out. Consider things like the specific meeting location ("Meet us near the large tree on the southwest corner of the park"); safety and access at your meeting location (Is there a public restroom? A safe and comfortable place to gather? Bus stops nearby?); the pace and duration of your walking and rolling experience (What would be a good length? What is your pace versus the pace of someone younger, older, or in a wheelchair?); breaks and resting areas along the route (Are there benches? Are there public restrooms? Is the full route accessible? Are there areas with shade?); what people might need (Will they benefit from having comfortable shoes for a dirt or gravel path? Extra water?). You do not need to make this route perfect. You do not need to overthink this. The more you care for the route itself, the more your participants will feel seen and the more they will be able to relax, open up, and connect alongside new and unique people.

Invitation: Once you have scouted your route and feel good about specifics, craft your invitations using whatever tools you are comfortable with (flyers, word of mouth, email, social media, bulletin boards, phone calls, local papers). Try to communicate as many details as you can but also be mindful of too much text. Give your invitation a clever, catchy name and make sure you add contact information (email and phone) so you can be reached with questions or in case someone cannot find you on the day of your event.

Circling Up: On Walk2Connect-inspired experiences, we start and finish with a circle. This anchors our movement in connection, story, and togetherness. In the starting circle, begin by welcoming everyone, introducing yourself, and offering meaningful inclusion statements and land acknowledgments. From there, invite everyone to go around (perhaps with some stretching and deep breathing) and share their names, where they are from, something that inspires them, and perhaps why they signed up for the event. You could also have fun icebreaking prompts that lighten the mood. The closing circle honors your movement before everyone takes off. I will often have everyone share one or two things that they learned or enjoyed. It is also an opportunity for people to share any announcements they might have.

Nurturing Comfort, Connection, and Movement: Hosting connection-focused walking or rolling experiences is never the same because each experience weaves different people on different days in new and different environments. Checking in on your people throughout your route is key to maintaining comfort, care, safety, and connection. Pause frequently to let people catch up to the whole group. Unless you are doing a more meditative walk or a longer-distance walk, your group will more than likely be in plenty of conversation. At your pause points, check in with people on their comfort and needs. Communicate flexibility throughout your movement so it is clear that the health of the whole is primary to your experience. I also really enjoy breaking up any default pairing. When you start moving, people will either self-select into moving with someone they know or who they end up next to in the starting circle. Every twenty minutes or so, when you pause to check in, encourage your group to "switch it up" and move with someone new. This is such a helpful nudge or invitation that inspires ongoing connection with a wide variety of people.

Extra Safety Notes: Take extra care when coming up to and crossing streets. Wear bright clothes and have a first-aid kit, extra water, and some simple snacks with you just in case. If you happen to be on a road with little or no sidewalks, make sure your group is moving against traffic so you can choose to get out of the way if cars aren't paying attention. It is best practice for bikes and runners to go with traffic and pedestrians to go against.

Time: Plan for at least forty-five to ninety minutes for most experiences. Longer distance and some themed and exploratory experiences will of course go longer.

First-Time Location Suggestion: If hosting something like this is new for you, I recommend having your first experience or two at a local public park. They usually have flat sidewalks or paths, public restrooms, shade, places to rest, and a predictable route looping around the park, or ways to turn back easily if needed.

2

WALKING AS HUMILITY

THIS COULD BE THE END

It was day 31 on our cross-country walk. We were on one of West Virginia's beautiful ridge highways, the 250 Waynesburg Pike, walking just east of Moundsville. As we moved, I was awestruck with the view. All around me was a sea of rolling hills and storybook farms.

The shoulders on these old roads were practically nonexistent; six inches at most. Imagine my six-foot-four frame with a huge backpack and a ninety-pound wolf dog trying to navigate ditches, puddles, canals, mud, bushes, mature tree roots, and numerous fences skirting the edges of a high-speed rural highway. While the views were breathtaking, I had to keep my attention almost solely on the road and countless split-second decisions to avoid getting hit by oncoming traffic.

As we pressed on toward Moundsville, the turns were getting sharper, and the slopes off the no-shoulder road were getting steeper. We were soon walking uphill on the highway in the actual lane of oncoming traffic. It was clear to my body that we were soon approaching an extremely dangerous turn. My instincts and my deep intuition were getting stronger and more tuned in each day into this journey. I was constantly scanning my environment for threats. As we approached the sharp turn, I steered all my attention toward our options for footing, dodging barriers, and darting to the other side when the shoulder disappeared.

To our left was a too-tall-to-climb-and-hop chain-link fence literally up against the road. To our right was a very steep drop where one would fall directly onto homes, trees, and farming equipment. Both options were terribly unsafe.

"Shit."

Okay. Back to the fence option. It was awful. Literally right up against the road, and even if I could hop over, how on Earth would I get Kanoa over it? Plus there was a large "Beware of Dogs" sign. I didn't see any dogs yet, but it didn't help. This was awful. I felt horribly stuck.

Okay. Back to the slope option. There was a break in traffic, and we hustled to the other side. I peered over as far as I could see. The drop was intense, and the slope was so steep that I actually couldn't make out what was in between the edge of my vantage point and actual ground. It felt too far and way too risky. I had so much weight, and I knew Kanoa would not willingly let go. He would push and pull and make my ability to hold ground for us both nearly impossible.

We're still moving. Since we aren't in the heart of the turn yet, oncoming traffic—mostly cars and small trucks—are pressing their brakes and weaving around us. As we approached what will forever be pedestrian hell in my bones, I lost all visibility to oncoming traffic from both sides. My heart started racing. My hands started trembling. My life. My dog. All the people in my life who I love and adore started flashing through my mind.

"We should go back.

No, we got this!

We should go back.

Fucking cars.

Fucking road designs.

We might die."

I kept mumbling back and forth as we started walking as fast as we could into the turn. We were lucky at the beginning not to have any cars. I kept stopping to listen for any traffic since I couldn't see anything.

Once we were perpendicular to the house inside the chain link fence, a rush of strong young bulldogs came running from the front door. They barked and yelped and spat with one sole purpose: to get a rise out of Kanoa. He was barking. They were barking. We were in the heart of the turn and pushed up, touching the fence as we took our steps. Kanoa was between my legs to avoid the chaos from the dogs.

"These dogs? Now? Really?"

They proceeded to bite and nip through the devilish fence. Our entire bodies were in this small two-lane rural highway. I was pleading and praying hard for no oncoming traffic.

Cars started to creep up behind us. Then I heard it. A faint and quickly increasing, "Br-r-gh" came from ahead.

My heart sank.

This was not a car.

We started running.

We ran as fast as we could with my clunky backpack and a tired and trembling body. The rushing semitruck saw us and was going too fast to stop. He started laying on his horn, as if that would do anything. The only options were to run to the other side and risk falling off the edge, or to force Kanoa between my body and the fence. I quickly and aggressively grabbed my ninety-pound dog with everything I had and squished us both into the fence and into the wet and teethy mouths of the yapping dogs. They were biting my hands, cheeks, Kanoa's ears, and anything they could. I felt like I was in a tornado. The truck was beeping and screaming for us to do something else, and all I could think about was surviving and throwing bull dogs. I started screaming as it got closer. "Ah-h-h!" My backpack and walking poles scraped the body of the truck as it blasted by.

I slowly blinked and took a breath. We were alive. We survived. I didn't have any time to reflect or recover. We ran as fast as we could to get to a better area where we could sit and see again.

We found a grassy shoulder, still on private property, but with no chain link fence. I cried, cleaned our dog-bite wounds, and sat in deep gratitude for being alive and the horror of what so many pedestrians face on any given day.

FRAGILE MOMENTS

My soft organs grabbing onto the fence with all that I had. Kanoa, full of soft organs, pressed against my chest and the fence. We were only inches away from being flattened on the pavement. We all have moments and perhaps, tiny or not so tiny miracles in our lives where, if we would have done one or two things differently, we would no longer be here. What in our lives keeps us close to our fragility? What in our lives draws out humbling perspectives that remind us, anchor us, and teach us illusions of certainty and control? When I think about my trembling body, bulldogs tearing away at my fingers, and the truck scraping my backpack, it is clear I had no control, no way out.

When we walk or roll with more intention and more often, we are putting our fragile human frame in more direct contact with the whims of the outside world. While this may initially seem like a negative, it is painfully important to see it as a necessary tool to keep us closer to one another, to the preciousness of moments, and to the great unknowns that live all around us. Our actual bodies moving on a wild, beautiful, and fierce planet is a humble, fragile, emergent, and courageous act.

FALLING AND RISING

Each step, each roll, is an act of agency to live, to exist, to try, and ultimately, to survive one more moment. Whether you move on two feet or in a wheelchair, gravity still wants us down. Imagine if we more intentionally acknowledged and honored that the Earth is constantly pulling us downward, down to its core. It is also important to acknowledge and honor that our bodies are constantly fighting and risking to keep us awake, upright, and alive. The specific relationship to falling and rising, with each step or roll, is profound as we consider walking as humility.

Invite, also, what my friend Antonia Malchik, author of *A Walking Life,* shares on the vestibular system,

> The vestibular system, in essence, tunes our physical bodies to the planet's center of gravity, a relationship so delicate and precise that it almost feels like magic. It's an incredible realization. When you walk across the room, it's your vestibular system that directs you where you want to go, or keeps you upright if you suddenly change direction. While we walk (or roll) down the road or run across a field or hike over a mountain ridge or nip up subway stairs, it's as if our bodies are chattering to Earth and listening intently to its responses (Malchik 2020, 29).

Imagine how we might better treat others and all living things if we had a more moment-by-moment reminder that we are, always, one step or roll from falling.

CIRCLES OF WASTE

There you are with your curled back, pants down, and hands on your forehead. You breathe out a sign of relief as you have just released a few solid stools. You made it before it came trickling down. The smells and the textures. The posture and the frumped nature of it all.

There is so much around us that tells us we need to constantly separate ourselves from our waste. Flush it. Bury it. Toss it. Get rid of it. I have a compost toilet in my mostly off-grid tiny home. Every time I use it, I am tangibly reminded of my body and its relationship to excrement. Every other month or so, I unhook the bucket and haul it to a place where I bury it. It is an important and always humbling experience for me to, yes, smell and carry my shit.

Nature and the universe have no interest in your desire for a private and tidy restroom experience. When you need to go, you need to go. How are your surroundings and the culture you find yourself in accepting of and even honoring of this plain-as-day human activity? What feeds false ideas of feeling or appearing superior to another related to keeping one's restroom experience private and tidy? Might our relationship to our waste be a portal to radical humility, healing, and belonging across all our lines, walls, and divides?

INTEGRATION PRACTICE:
PUBLIC RESTROOM AWARENESS

As you move,* be extra mindful of your own restroom needs. As you near needing to use the restroom, pay attention to where and how this experience is valued, honored, understood, and protected by your city, state, neighborhood, local businesses, and the general public. When or if you find a place to use the restroom, notice how you are treated and the overall dignity of this experience. Do you need to buy something? Is it close, safe, accessible, and easy to use?

---

* If you walk or roll as your primary form of transportation and you experience the injustice of public restroom availability, dignity, and accessibility, learn who in your town or community is working on behalf of public health and public safety. Share your stories with them.

Take notes on how certain parks, transit stations, bus stops, and commercial areas could better accommodate public restroom needs. You might also come up with creative invitations to engage local businesses and organizations to become friends and sponsors of the public restroom experience.

WE WILL NEVER REALLY KNOW

It was especially quiet on the roads until about 12 p.m. as all the local churches let out. It was also Easter Sunday. It was day 35 on my cross-country walk, and we were moving between Barnesville and Quaker City, Ohio. Several people drove up next to Kanoa and I with their arms out the window. They would wave and look at us with curiosity. I started to pick up that this would happen pretty frequently on Sundays at this time. A good look up and down, a small grin and often a full elbow out of the window followed up by, "You saved yet, boy? Do you know Jesus? Do you know our Lord?"

I am sometimes entertained and sometimes annoyed by these requests. Some feel caring and genuine. Others not so much. As someone who moved through complex seasons of Christian faith expression, I am in no position to judge. I am, however, far less patient when someone's self-worth, relationship to love, and sense of belonging are manipulated and harmed by people practicing any one religion. I literally feel sick in my stomach when I sense that people believe they have the moral authority over my relationship to the Divine, God, Nature, Universe, Great Mystery, Spacious Unknown. More than anything, I wish that folks who stay in their cars (or behind their walls) would leave the safety of artificial walls and walk with me for a few hours. We could offer and listen to one another's story, allowing love and connection to more naturally blossom from there.

As I continued down the road, a large red pickup truck pulled over. An older woman with full rosy cheeks was driving. She very quickly invited me and Kanoa to come up to the window. I was starting to drum up creative ideas to what I assumed would be Jesus-talk. Kanoa jumped up with his huge wolf paws. She jumped, but as I told him to get down, she said, "Oh, you're fine, we're in the country. Dogs are always jumping on our trucks."

"Listen, I am in a hurry to make it back to my home. I have to finish preparing our Easter meal," she said. "I feel a little uneasy about it, but I just can't bear to have you out here on your own on Easter Sunday."

She offered to take Kanoa and I in the bed of the pickup truck to her home, where the whole family would be gathered. She needed me to decide fast. It took two seconds for me to look at the ground, look at Kanoa, and then back to her. "Wow. Thank you for this invitation! Would you be open to driving us back to this spot after our meal?" I asked.

"Of course! Now get in the back."

Homemade food? Rest? Restroom? Water fill-up? We didn't hesitate and jumped in the bed of her truck. Off we went. We continued chatting through the open slot between the bed of the truck and her front seat. As we drove, she hopped on her phone quickly to let one of her daughters know that she was picking up a stray.

"You know that young man we saw walking after church?" she whispered, trying not to make me feel uncomfortable.

"Yes, him! He's with me in the bed of the truck with his dog. They are both very sweet. I'm nervous, but I just had to stop and invite him."

I heard high-pitched sounds on the other end.

"Mom! Are you serious?"

"Yes. We're almost there," she noted.

You could tell she was a bit stressed and unsure. You could also tell this was a woman who trusted her gut. The way the family talked about it later, it was clear that moments like these weren't too far from the norm.

We arrived, and the younger kids were kicking around a ball; the older kids with their partners and friends were seated around picnic tables outside. They had a simple and cozy ranch-like backyard and a humble one-story home that you could tell had been in the family for years. They were surrounded by a large, mature forest.

As we jumped out of the bed of the truck, with my poles and large backpack, I noticed the siblings looking at one another and shaking their heads with a smirk. It was awkward for them to know how to greet me, so I charged in and put my hand out to say hi. Kids quickly came rushing up to Kanoa. This dog and his goofy lop-eared magic. He makes everything easier.

Within minutes I had a beer in my hand while connecting with a few of the family members. We enjoyed amazing food, and I had such a meaningful time sharing the holiday with a new and special rural Ohio family. The grandmother, the one who picked me up, came up to me after the meal. She invited me into her living room.

Before dropping me back off, she wanted to share something with me. She picked up a bowl of varied colored rocks. She looked at me and then looked away as if to hide tears. She was trying to get out the words, but her inability to hold back emotion was keeping the words from coming out. If you could only see the softness of her round face and the colors shifting from white to pink to red. I saw that other family members were aware of what was going on. They too began to shed tears. Their hands were on one another's shoulders as they remained huddled in the kitchen. I waited patiently and gave her as much time as needed.

She apologized every five seconds. I kept affirming her that it was okay. I eventually put my hand on her shoulder to let her know that I was not uncomfortable by her emotion. As I did, one of her daughters came in and did the same. The grandmother took a deep breath and looked directly into my eyes.

"It is such a joy for us to have you here, to share Easter together.

"We are all so encouraged and inspired by what you are doing.

"You will see things that some of us can only dream to see.

"Our family has gone through a lot this year already, and this Easter is especially hard for us.

"Do you see this picture?" she slowly walked over to the other side of the room and grabbed a framed picture of a blond teenage man. He was smiling and leaning against the open passenger side of what seemed to be his car.

She pressed her hand onto the glass covering the photo. She teared up again, looked away, and handed me the photo.

"My grandson, Jasen ...

"He ..."

More tears ...

"This is the first holiday family gathering where he ..."

More time ...

"Jasen took his own life two months ago, Jonathon."

My heart sank.

"It's simply been a heart-wrenching experience for all of us. We are all still taking it day by day. We have no idea why or what was so hard for him. We miss and love him terribly."

I was now looking deeper and deeper into this snapshot of time. Jasen was growing with family and friends. There was a squint in his eye that reminded me of my own. He leaned on his car with a baggy shirt and seemed to be carrying himself like any other teenager in his time. My mind and heart were swirling. What pressures and projections did he carry from friends, family, and society? Would his faith community welcome, embrace, and comfort all that was happening on this inside? What wounds, stories, or secrets tormented him? Who did he confide in?

At this point, her daughters were in the room, and they all had their arms around one another. Tears continued to flow.

"Would you do us a favor?" asked the grandmother.

Tears were now swelling in my eyes. "Of course I will. I am so deeply sorry for your loss. What a special young man ... what on Earth would ..." were the first fumbled words out of my mouth.

"As I saw you walking on the road, I felt Jasen walking with you. As I heard you talk about your travels, I felt Jasen sitting next to you, enthralled by what you were doing and dreaming to do something similar. I saw him bombarding you with excitement, curiosity, and questions.

"Would you be so kind as to take a handful of these rocks and leave them in some of the most beautiful places on your journey, as a symbol of Jasen's life to us and to everyone he touched—a symbol of Jasen's spirit in some of God's most beautiful landscapes?"

Tears flowed from my face. I was overwhelmed with love and understanding for this grandmother, for the family, and for Jasen. My own trembling journey with suicide came rushing to the surface in their living room. The aches. The pain. The miracle of surviving it.

"You have my word.

"I will take these rocks, and in prayer and remembrance will leave them in places that are beyond words. Thank you for trusting me with them."

A HUMBLE WAY

Take a few moments to pause and reflect on this story. I invite you to take a couple of deep breaths. As you bring attention to your breath, honor the lives of all who feel and face such life-altering heartbreak. Be with and honor the depths and complexities of what others carry.

As the story above illustrates, we will never fully know what it is like to be in the shoes and breath of another. The vastness of what could never be fully known aches for more humility. Let's try slowly holding the mirror up. Do you know, without question, what exactly is taking place inside of you?

Did you know the Latin roots of the word *humility* are *humus:* "earth," and *humilitas:* "to the ground"? With this context, and in my own experience, I find that moving in an unhurried way on everyday streets, under rolling clouds, and in more natural sight of all living creatures we share this planet with, is inherently humble. This one-step-or-roll-at-a-time modality almost immediately moves us into more nonlinear relationships. It brings our bodies into the whims of our surroundings, into the nuanced spaces between weakness and strength, courage and powerlessness, right and wrong, agency and meekness, and so much more. Walking in a humble way invites these complexities to pull and tug at one another.

INTEGRATION PRACTICE: KNOWING AND UNKNOWING

Wherever you are, I invite you to slowly begin walking or rolling. It could be around your room, in a hallway, or outside.

With one step or roll, I invite you to say to yourself, "I'm not actually sure."

With the other step or roll, I invite you to say to yourself, "I trust my life experience."

One, "The way is uncertain."

Two, "I trust the path I am on."

One, "I don't know."

Two, "I do know."

State these invitations several times with gentle repetition. What begins to come up in you? Where do you feel inspiration? Where do you feel blocked? Move with compassion and grace, however it lands. As you continue moving, practice offering these expressions in relation to people in your life.

What about my unhurried and humble frame moving on the road on Easter Sunday made me accessible to the beloved grandmother who stopped to pick me up? What about my unhurried humble movement opened my heart, senses, and neuro network to be spacious and open with people who believed and lived differently than me? Rabbi Nilton Bonder (2010) writes:

> Many people believe that humility is the opposite of pride, when, in fact, it is a point of equilibrium. The opposite of pride is actually a lack of self-esteem. A humble person is totally different from a person who cannot recognize and appreciate himself (herself, themselves) as part of this world's marvels.

You and I are capable of causing tremendous harm when looking at people and creation through a magnifying glass, ready to zap anything that threatens us or doesn't fit into our limited vantage points. If we are ever to be on an authentic healing journey of humility, we must face how we project power, shame, fear, and perfection onto others. I find that slowly moving can be a compassionate way to spend time with our own shortcomings, weaknesses, mistakes, gaps, and questions.

INTEGRATION PRACTICE:
WALKING STICK

During your next walk, I invite you to use, borrow, or pick up a walking stick (preferably wooden). Move with it as a reminder that (a) you are always one turn or fall away from death and dust, and (b) trees, soil, and all created things are with you and woven into your deep existence. Imagine this stick as an additional channel to the Earth, the ground. Walking sticks can also give off the impression that you are in need of extra support; therefore, not to have a walking stick would infer that you are not in need of support. Using a walking stick can invite, with humility and care, a practice around acknowledging and accepting that we are always in need of and benefiting from support: from loved ones, the planet, ancestors, and one's sense of soul, spirit, and cosmic connection.

DEDICATED PRACTICE

Take some time to move with the practice below. Do you know the Indigenous tribal lands you are walking or rolling on? Learn from and honor them as you move. Listen to your body. Honor your needs. Honor the lived reality of all who walk or use a wheelchair as their primary form around you. Honor what will work for you, especially depending on your ability, community, and context. No rules. Only invitation.

To Know the Ground

Somewhere along the way, many of us were told to "Get up off the ground!" or "Look, act, or be presentable!" While these statements meet us all in unique places, they can too often justify dehumanization related to those who sit on the ground, those who have dirt on their shoes, and those who do not look presentable, whatever "presentable" means. While ideas of cleaning up and wiping off the mud can create a healthy sense of confidence and empowerment, it can quickly turn into another form of separation. Are we all not messy people who came from the dirt and will go back to the dirt? It is also important to name that ongoing systemic racism, classism, and treatment of homelessness can feed situations of social, spatial, emotional, and physical violence for those who don't "get up off the ground and get in line."

Invitation: For this practice, I am inviting you, as often as you can while on your walk,* to sit or lie on the grass, on the curb, and on the dirt. No need for a bench or a rock unless you need or want one. Find your own way to increase your proximity to the soil, to the Earth's core. From there, explore what is around you as you sit, kneel, or lie down. Feel the sand, dirt, rocks, soil, and pavement. Notice the details in small plants that reach to grow and survive. Get to know them. Revisit them. Scan your environment, around and above you, from this vantage point. Invite awareness and openness for how being upright or quickly moving through the world feeds stories of disconnection and superiority to all who depend on the ground for rest, for sleep, for food, for prayer and ceremony, and much more.

Whether you are in a wheelchair or sitting/lying on the ground, you might ask and reflect on the following questions. You might write them down so you can easily read them to yourself and out loud:

- Am I feeling connected to the Earth? Why or why not?

- What am I thinking about or feeling as I sit or lay down? Others? Discomfort? Fear? Inspiration? Connection? Disconnection?

- Am I noticing sounds, smells, details, and perspectives from this vantage point? People, buildings, traffic, exhaust, stones, sticks, flowers, sky, community, insects?

- How am I connecting to my body and the theme of humility?

Adaptation 1. Going Barefoot: Moving while barefoot—on soil, on streets, on grass, on all environments—can intentionally connect us to how our actual skin interacts with the actual ground as it is. Sharper objects can

---

* If you are in a wheelchair, powered scooter, or position of discomfort related to getting down on the ground itself, I invite you to find a place to pause, observe, feel, and check in on how the "walking or rolling as humility" invitation moves with you on a day-to-day basis or in the particulars of this moment. Take some time to creatively reflect through journaling, storytelling, poetry, sketching, or audio or spoken word.

sting or puncture our exterior. Soft soil can help hold the weight of our often tired and forgotten bodies. Moving in this way over time can also strengthen calluses on our skin to help us withstand tension and pain. Keep in mind that many feet may not physically be able to walk or move at any great length in this way. This practice is just as profound when going in small and more careful circles in a yard or park. If you go barefoot for too long when getting started, you risk injuring your foot in significant ways. Be extra mindful of your limitations and needs.

Location: Start where you live or work. Try to sit or lie directly on the ground, or as near to it as you can. Move in your community and sit in your front yard, or an area just off the roadway, maybe right on the cracks of a sidewalk, the curb of a quieter street corner, the middle of a park or field, or whatever calls out to you.

3

WALKING AS A HUMAN RIGHT

I'M STILL SHAKING

Twenty of us are gathered just a few blocks from the large intersection of West Colfax and Federal Boulevard in Denver. We are standing in a circle next to one another outside a local library. We are away from meeting rooms, computer screens, living rooms, and cars. Our group is a diverse mix of residents, media, and representatives from public housing, the City of Denver, the Colorado Department of Transportation (CDOT), and local nonprofits. As with all Walk2Connect events, we start in a circle. We begin with introductions, set intentions, go over safety guidance, and offer a summary of what to expect throughout our experience. Most people in the group, except for residents, have never fully walked or rolled the practical route we are about to experience. Most people in this circle do not live in the neighborhood; however, everyone has a role in influencing decisions made on behalf of those who walk, use a wheelchair, or ride the bus here.

We start walking east from the library toward what is called the Colfax Clover, which is a high-speed four-way on- and off-ramp intersection shaped like a four-leaf clover.

Colfax, the longest commercial corridor east to west in the United States, intersects here with Federal Boulevard, the deadliest road, specific to pedestrian-automobile crashes, in the city of Denver (Roberts 2021). There is high-volume foot, wheelchair, and bus traffic as it also connects to the Federal light-rail station. While there are planning improvements coming, a blatant disconnect is the newly erected (in 2018) CDOT office building, which sits right on the corner of this hostile intersection. Other than one attached sidewalk, there are nearly zero supports for people who walk, roll, and take the bus surrounding the new building. Cars fly by in all directions, and everyone outside of cars is isolated and largely disregarded. Seeing the large "Colorado Department of Transportation" sign on the building next to a large covered parking garage affirms ongoing systemic distrust.

We continue moving. I frequently share that there are several practical destinations nearby: a library, a human resources center, a recreation center, a mental health center, public housing, schools, and parks. I want all involved to center their awareness around those who use these environments without a choice all hours of the day and in all conditions. They are not just old, cracked sidewalks. They are not just diagonal ramps that happen to leave strollers and wheelchairs in the wake of 40- to 60-mile-per-hour traffic. They are oppressive, hostile, and even violent lived realities.

Just a few blocks in, participants are made painfully aware of how hard it is to navigate the broken, thin, not-really-sidewalks that hug the high-speed off-ramps coming from busy Federal Boulevard. There is a blind turn to oncoming cars, a large bush that pushes most of us onto the road, and an unavoidable high-speed crossing over the off-ramp itself. Within minutes, it is clear to everyone, in their body, that they feel unsafe, unprotected, and even devastated by the gaps and tragedies facing today's human body around one of the busiest intersections in the city. As we huddle under a large, daunting, and oppressive concrete overpass, a participant shares, "I'm still shaking from that last crossing."

When you walk or roll, things more naturally open in the heart and body. This helps to make more room to feel, absorb, and ingest one's experience. Your senses are turned all the way up.

In our huddle, I make it clear that this is not a walking tour. It is a kinetic experience rooted in body-based education related to what people go through on a day-to-day basis. Keeping safety in mind, I highly encourage participants to document their unique experience through taking photos, writing notes, and recording audio or video. I invite them to specifically reference how they feel, what they encounter, and the details of the built environment around them.

We continue moving under the overpass. We are fully encased by the noise and speed of rush-hour traffic. It is loud and deafening. No benches, no public restrooms, no lights, no welcoming places where nature or even people can thrive. I ask the group to stop and really feel the inhumanity and separation of it all. Allow the noises to fill your ears. Allow the smell of exhaust to fill your nose. Allow the rush and chaos of it all to open and awaken new and needed things within.

As we continue moving, I ask:

"What are the social, communal, and environmental costs of taking car-centric transportation as far as we have?

"How are we making proximity to nature available to all and not just those who drive?

"How would one's overall mental and physical health improve if they could breathe cleaner air and more comfortably process stress while they walk or roll?

"Would transportation systems become more people- and planet-friendly if those who make decisions on these very systems spent more time walking, rolling, and using the bus for transportation?"

As we make our way up onto Federal Boulevard, I point out a steep foot-trodden dirt path, or in planning speak, a "desire line." A desire line shows practical behavior related to where people actually need or want to go. It might be steep and even dangerous in mud or rain, but it is much more convenient than a long paved path winding them away from the bus stop, grocery store, or destination.

Some of us make our way up the desire line, and others go around the long, winding sidewalk. Once on top, everyone notices there is no crossing if we wanted to take the bus southbound, and how far it is from any safe light or protected crossing to get there. I stop the group and ask them to imagine all the darting that takes place here. Just before we continue, we all witness an elderly woman holding two bags of groceries waiting in the middle of the street for a break in traffic. She is isolated and terribly exposed to hundreds of vehicles moving at such high-speeds.

We keep moving southbound until we get to the next traffic light to cross. As we wait, we witness over fifty people waiting for their first bus, regrouping after getting off the most recent bus, or waiting for their connecting bus. This is across the street from the new CDOT office building. I ask the group to see if they notice any seating, public restrooms, food vendors, or anything that would be remotely relaxing or nourishing. I also remind people, as I do throughout the walk, to invite imagery of nighttime, families and children, heavy rain, snow, and ice.

We keep moving.

Broken or nonexistent sidewalks push us right up to the road. We are now moving southbound. Traffic flies just inches behind and beside us. We assume and hope that the hundreds of drivers who move in our midst are focused enough to not swerve just a yard to the right. The paths that people try to walk are often blocked by parked cars, are bent at an angle into the street, or are simply absent. This, in all hours of the day, forces pedestrians and people who use wheelchairs to move directly into traffic or to navigate private property. As participants take all of this in, two parents pushing their babies in strollers squeeze by us just as the most active bus on Federal (every fifteen minutes) roars by just inches away.

Everyone takes a deep breath.

We continue to pass bus stops, liquor stores, gas stations, grocery markets, taco stands, restaurants, and clinics. I ask everyone the following question: Why are roads that have higher concentrations of public housing and practical destinations the most hostile to those who depend on walking, rolling, and transit? I ask them to feel and move with this question and the many systemic gaps impacting equity in transportation specific to class, race, and corporate interests.

We keep moving. People who see us and move by us wave, smile, and show curiosity at the sight of our large collective. The smells of street-side cooking and all the friendly faces we see along this journey remind us that even in horrendous conditions, the human spirit is vibrant and very much alive.

As we make our way back, I have everyone in our group take the Federal Boulevard bus northbound. More than half the group had never taken the bus.

Toward the end of the walk, one of the participants from the CDOT team came up to me. She said, "You know, back toward the beginning when you said that it's not right for transportation departments and community organizations to describe walking as a choice, I didn't agree with you. Now, after this walk, I deeply get it. For twenty years I have had an intellectual relationship with transportation. Until now. Thank you for what you are doing and what you are teaching us."

INTEGRATION PRACTICE:
ADVOCATING FOR OUR STREETS

If we want to challenge or influence transportation systems—specifically sidewalks, bus stops, transit routes, accessibility, intersections, roads, parks, and trails—it is extremely helpful to research and understand the agencies and individuals that plan, budget, develop, manage, and maintain them. It is also helpful to know if there are organizations, groups, or local and regional campaigns that are already advocating for things you care about. You might go right into research by searching online, visiting your local library, asking neighbors, or making phone calls to your city, county, or state office. Before your research, take notes of specific streets, intersections, crossings, or greenways that you want to learn more about. This can be a great starting place for reporting gaps in the system and for organizing walks and rolls that help educate, challenge, and engage these very agencies and the greater community. Examples: city, county, and state agencies such as public works, planning, public health, recreation, public housing, sustainability, or the state transportation department; public officials in your district such as city council, state representatives, the mayor's office, county commissioners; local advocacy organizations for transit, safe streets, accessibility, pedestrian safety, or biking; and community health networks.

WE ARE NOT STIFF, ARTIFICIAL OBJECTS

When we step or roll outside, we open our senses, our bodies, and our inner dimensions to a universe of unpredictable elements. As we continue moving, however slow or fast, whether on a familiar path or one that unfolds, we begin to integrate our own story with the story of what is around us. This detail, the interfolding of it all, where the collective weaves together with the one, is something I find so deeply compelling about moving in this way. More wise words from Antonia's *A Walking Life:*

> How our public spaces are created and maintained, how we use them, and who gets to use them without repercussions makes a difference to the health of our neighborhoods, towns, and nations. Walking is both a cornerstone of a functional society, and a deeply political act in its own right (Malchik 2020, 64).

Literally *driving* away from this inherent human embodiment has and continues to create devastating conditions on human minds, hearts, bodies, and communities. Even in places all over the world where walking is still the primary form of transportation, the car is becoming the rule of success, upward mobility, and efficiency. Creative agency around the complex effects of what can so quickly become an all-consuming fifty- or sixty-mile-per-hour way of moving, relating, and being in the world is needed more than ever. Jeff Speck's *Walkable City* is an important book rooting into how our planning, engineering, and policy have left us scrambling in a deep car-centric crisis. He says,

> Long gone are the days when automobiles expanded possibility and choice for the majority of Americans. Now, thanks to its ever-increasing demands for space, speed, and time, the car has reshaped our landscape and lifestyles around its own needs (Speck 2013, 75).

Whether we like it or not, we are not stiff, artificial objects. We are moving, dynamic, flexible, fluid creatures who depend on our capacity to adapt and learn from our environment. It is a human right to develop one's brain, heart, body, social networks, and sense of place at an unhurried pace. When we blindly celebrate and design everyday places around high-speed, motorized,

three-thousand-pound-plus tin boxes that can kill a human body
within seconds, then, at bare minimum, we should have places to
walk or roll that are protected, safe, comfortable, equitable, and
even enjoyable.

The automobile industry works day and night to dominate
our personal and collective psyche. For people who drive and have
always driven as their primary form of transportation, there is an
unquestionable, and for some, romantic, relationship to the car. I get
it. I gave my cars names. I petted them when they supported long
trips and took me to inspiring places. I understand this connection.
I am also awake to the trickery behind this complex relational gaze.
Everywhere I look, listen, or turn there are million-dollar efforts to
have you and me emotionally entangled in ads exalting the automobile as our unquestionable friend, as ultimate luxury, as infallible
convenience, and as playful happiness. What we don't gaze into is the
around-the-clock devastation of who or what gets lost or destroyed
along the way. What is the actual cost—overseas, in our community,
in our natural habitats, in our hearts—of this complex love affair?

A reminder that I am not car-shaming. I am highlighting the
harm of cars existing and remaining at the center of all transportation behaviors and systems. Like anything we cling to, we will
fiercely, consciously or unconsciously, defend it, even if it is destroy-
ing our own bodies, minds, relationships, and ecosystems.

DISTANCE, TIME, AND FEAR

We need systems to change. We need federal, state, city, and county
agencies to radicalize their relationship to transportation to center
accessibility, rolling, walking, taking transit, and biking. We need
public-serving, policy-making leaders to propose, organize, and
push bills that radically reorient our transportation systems around
our physical and mental health, social connection, and Earth stewardship. We also need leaders and the public showing up with

more awareness, urgency, integrity, and equity with stories, heart, and creativity. I believe that for more of us to more genuinely show up, we must take more risks to live it, feel it, and experience it frequently and in a variety of seasons and conditions.

If driving is your primary form of transportation, I encourage you and your family, neighborhood, and organizations to make more room in your bodies, hearts, and minds for the following questions and invitations. If you already walk or roll as your primary form, I invite you to share these invitations with your car-driving peers and people in positions that impact your transportation and public health experience.

"I live too far from where I need to go."

- Commit to one car per household. Compromise convenience with shared trips and not as many trips.

- Organize immediate neighbors around carpooling to town, the store, school, and so on. Not every individual needs to take separate cars to do all the things.

- Advocate around public transit options near you. Are there any? How often do they run? Poll or survey your community or neighborhood around need, access, and involvement.

- Begin parking fifteen minutes, thirty minutes, or even an hour away, via foot or wheelchair, from your various destinations or transit stop.

"I don't have time."

- I hear you, especially related to longer distances. While layers of systemic injustice and unsustainable land-use development impact and devastate our sense of time, I invite all of us to get creative with how we take time back. Reorient your relationship to transportation like you make time for other practical appointments, events, or activities. You make the time because you make it a priority. Start with one practical trip per week, or per month, replaced fully or partially by walking, rolling, or transit. See what grows and blossoms from there.

- Organize a local campaign with students and people who can't legally, medically, or physically drive to encourage your local public officials to commit to a week without driving, replacing all trips with walking, rolling, and transit.

"I am afraid, and I don't feel safe."

- This is painfully real. Fear and safety make these invitations complex and tender, especially when we consider race, gender, ability, religious or spiritual expression, age, and sexual orientation. Try inviting someone, or a small group of people, to move with you. Maybe this invitation is specific to trying on full or partial routes to common destinations, or maybe it is just a walking and rolling group to start. Have phone numbers of friends on hand, and consider scouting possible routes by bike, bus, or car beforehand. Take a self-defense course and get a good walking stick. Treat your transportation like you would any event, trip, or activity that requires constructive thought around navigating one's comfort and safety.

You might slowly reread the points above. Honor your unique needs related to ability and safety. Write down ideas that are specific to your body, lived reality, neighborhood, workplace, or family patterns. As you jot down ideas, take them with you on a walk or roll. Try not to see them as only a list of ideas. Try with all you have to move into action. Allow them to challenge and inspire your day-to-day transportation behaviors.

INTEGRATION PRACTICE:
ONE–MILE RADIUS

If driving is your primary form of transportation and you live in a city, town, or suburban area, I invite you to mark or locate your home or place of residence on a map, online or on paper. If you are online, be sure the map is capturing streets, parks, and practical destinations that are one or two miles away. From there, print the map and draw a one- or two-mile radius around your location. For a week, a month, or longer, if you are able, commit to only walk or roll within that one- or two-mile radius. If you are in a rural area, or if there are no practical destinations (school, workplace, library, grocery) within one or two miles of your home, create the radius around your workplace or any area that you might frequently visit. Get dropped off or begin to find new areas for parking your vehicle to only walk or roll within your committed area. Invite others to join. You might bike some of your routes beforehand. Be safe. Center and honor what it is like for all who walk or roll as their primary form of transportation.

Depending on your pace and environment:

1 mile: roughly 15 to 45 minutes

2 miles: roughly 30 to 90 minutes

VISUALIZATION: DRENCHED AND DEPLETED

You are walking or moving in a wheelchair. You are en route to catch the only bus that goes to where your medical appointment is. It runs every hour and sometimes doesn't show up at all. You know the buses in the early morning are more reliable. It rained heavy last night, and street medians, intersections, and paved-over watersheds are flooded. You are dodging, skirting around, or having to go right through the water. You get splashed by rushing high-speed traffic. Because of the flooding, you have to go slower than usual.

Your back hurts because you didn't sleep well.

Your shoulders hurt because it's not good for you to carry all these groceries.

Your glasses are fogged up and you can't wipe them.

You're angry because you slipped and a can of soup went rolling into the gutter.

Your mind is heavy because you are exhausted from the grind.

Your heart aches because you never seem to get enough time with loved ones.

Shit. You see the bus several blocks ahead. It is ten minutes early. The no-bench, no-shelter bus stop is full of people waiting. You see them start to get on. You panic. Maybe you can make it if they take their time. Yelling won't help. You can't wave your hands. You pick up your pace, clench your bags, hold your pain, and try.

There it goes. Everyone got on. Except you. You worked so hard to arrive early too. You knew the weather would be bad. You knew you had to be quick at the store.

The bus flies right by you, splashing you on the way. You tried to wave your arms, make a scene, and ignite sympathy from the driver. Not today. Not on most days. Cars continue to rush past you. No one sees you. Time turns to heavy mud. You must stand for the next hour and wait for the next bus, if it comes. No bench. No shelter. Drenched. Depleted. You could rest in a nearby café, but you have to buy something. You can't sit in the patch of thorny grass because it's soaked and would hurt your knees. You also need to use the restroom. Where could you possibly go? Hold it in. You will be shamed and fined if you go in public. Keep it in.

Pause for a moment. Allow this invitation to sink in and move with you. I invite you to take a deep breath all the way in and slowly out. You might slowly read this invitation again while moving (walking or rolling) right where you are. You might close your eyes and invite someone to read it aloud to you. How does it make you feel? Have you ever felt this way related to your transportation experience? Why or why not? How might class, race, health, ability, and time spent in an automobile influence or impact your reflection?

THE IMPORTANCE OF ONE VOICE

As noted in chapter 1, Pam Jiner is a longtime friend. We have cohosted and cocreated numerous walking events and pedestrian equity actions together. She is the director and founder of Montbello Walks and is the 2017 GirlTrek Organizer of the year. She is one of my heroes.

> I have lived in my community of Montbello in Denver, Colorado, for forty-nine years. I remember my childhood experience vividly. I rode my bike everywhere. As an adult, GirlTrek inspired me to start walking. As I started walking, I noticed that everything was the same, yet everything had also changed. Blocks were the same. Buildings were the same. No safety improvements and still no amenities like accessible sidewalks, bus shelters, benches, and trees. What had changed is that Montbello was no longer 96 percent Black. Over seventy thousand people had moved into our small community, and it had become 70 percent Mexican and other Latino. There were also more nationalities represented. We still had the same floods leaving cars and people stranded on popular streets. We had zero crosswalks and few stop signs. With more people needing to move through our community, the gaps made one's transportation experience even more stressful, unsafe, and violent.

> Everyone should have free access to trails, walking, and parks. I was aggravated. We need to open our eyes. The benefits of walking, when feeling safe and comfortable, are endless. It is an incredible stress outlet. I walk just about every day to release stress.

The health benefits make it a social justice issue. Give us the freedom to walk so we can get into our bodies. If we walk on a regular basis, we can practice better health on a daily basis. If we walk more in our community, we can meet and greet one another at the grocery store and at local parks on a daily basis. Relationships start to build. When we are speeding through streets and carrying too much stress, we tend not to recognize one another. I have a right to safely walk at the park, take a break on a bench, and connect with another parent. I have a right to build healthy relationships in my community.

Four years ago, I more intentionally started tracking these gaps and calling for change. I started by connecting with community members. We started weekly walks with seniors, neighbors, and community leaders. I invited others to walk with me. I documented all of our walks with photos, stories, and connection and shared them publicly to encourage others to join. On our walks I asked participants what they liked and didn't like.

It took getting frustrated and fed up that the problems were still here. Why hasn't any of this been fixed? Who is responsible? Who can help me fix it? As a GirlTrek Leader, I started inviting city council, registered neighborhood association members, community organizations, and more to join and help me strategize. I began identifying departments (wastewater and drainage, public works, parks and recreation, planning, the state department of transportation). I hosted several pedestrian safety audits with tools sponsored by GirlTrek. I would cohost walks with other groups like Walk2Connect and WalkDenver who agree with me and are working on similar issues.

When I first started inviting people from public agencies, they would send interns or entry-level staff members: someone who could not influence change. I would scout walking routes that told important stories of inequity, coordinate dates, help people plan, and support them with snacks. It felt like an injustice not to have actual decision-makers present. It was humiliating and heartbreaking enough to have to rewalk the danger and violence of these streets.

Why don't they care about me and my community? It is not right. It does not feel good in my body. I have had to walk over fields of dry mud or water for years. I have seen and have helped people on wheelchairs navigate impossible environments between our residential areas and a new transit station. We move on the side of hills to stay out of the street.

As people would experience what I and my community members experience, I noticed that many of them do care. They are just unaware. Why was it so normal for us to deal with it year after year? So many people moving through that mess. I used to stand up in the back seat of my mother's car and I would watch for the huge splash as we went through a small lake of a puddle on our most popular commercial street. I enjoyed it as a kid. As an adult, it was aggravating. All the accidents, access, and issues from backed-up water drains for well over fifty years.

Systemic racism is real.

Those at the top are selective about what communities they will improve. Where will they save money by not providing updated infrastructure? On those early walks, entry-level representatives said they would "look into it." In emails, phone calls, public meetings, and on many of our walks, transportation jargon felt like an intentional delay. They intentionally used language I wouldn't understand. When I pushed myself to learn it, to understand it, I invited them back out and used their own language. I have a clear problem and am putting a lot of time into organizing this invitation. If they cannot make decisions, why are you sending them? It would make me feel guilty to bring all this up. I should not feel guilty about something that has impacted the health of my community for so many years. I kept pushing. I kept inviting. I kept demanding that actual decision-makers join our walks.

Decision-makers finally started showing up and began taking notes and measurements. They would come back several times to study what was wrong. Within months, they fixed it. No more water buildup. On our walks, state, city, and public transit agency staff felt the violence of slippery mud paths next to a high-speed roadway. On our walks, state, city, and public transit agency staff felt the accessibility and safety gaps facing our most vulnerable community members, especially those accessing a new transit station. Significant improvements for sidewalks and access have been planned and even implemented since. We had a small celebration in the middle of a large construction project after new, wide, and flat sidewalks were put in under the highway. It is important to find joy and to celebrate!

I share all of this to name the importance of one voice.

It took fifty-four years for one person to say something to cause change. Public agencies, city council members, state agencies—everybody went through the flooding water. No one said anything about it. This is the power of one voice. I walked three generations of kids in this community: my kids, my foster kids, and my grandkids. We have to speak up about the things that make you feel crappy. We must invite people into what it feels like. We should be able to breathe and be proud of our community.

TRANSPORTATION JUSTICE: PUBLIC MOVEMENT AND EVERY BREATH

I invite you first to pause and take a deep breath to honor all that Pam has shared with us. Her story and the story of millions in this time make it imperative that race and class continue to be named. We must take more personal, public, and political risk to center what aches through all of Pam's examples.

Dr. Robert Bullard, professor of urban planning and environmental policy at Texas Southern University, shares,

> Historically, urban planners followed the path of least resistance. And because minority communities were already disenfranchised, they did not have a say in how their neighborhoods were developed.... Freeways and bus routes, however, are just one part of a bigger picture: what urban planners refer to as "locally unwanted land-uses." These projects include highways, landfills,

incinerators, bus depots, and other kinds of projects that dispro-
portionately fall in minority communities and often cause pollution and harm the health of residents (Valentine 2020).

The race and class divides are loud and blatant. When you move
through it all, you feel it. You feel a systemic disregard for all who
live and move through these spaces. Equity must make its way to the
center of all public agencies for our systems to have public integrity.

Urban planner and writer Angie Schmitt, in her book *Right of
Way*, adds:

> Too often, the agencies responsible for infrastructure decisions
> are not in tune with the needs of communities of color. One
> of the most dramatic examples of infrastructure inequality is
> the situation faced by Native Americans. Native people suffer
> the worst pedestrian safety outcomes of any racial group in the
> United States.... Indian reservations and tribal lands are typ-
> ically located in rural areas where roads lack elements that
> make them safe for walking such as sidewalks and crosswalks.
> Reservations, though, function a lot more like cities or small
> villages where many people rely on walking to get around,
> which means that tribal citizens and visitors are often forced
> to cross and walk along the shoulders of rural highways, right
> next to high-speed traffic from heavy trucks (Schmitt 2020, 38).

The ongoing systemic dehumanization of Indigenous people and
Black communities by way of generational wealth, land ownership, redlining, policing, oil interests, mental health, generational
trauma, education segregation and access, health-care access,
leadership representation, and predatory businesses and development must be radically integrated into all aspects of federal, state,
regional, and local transportation planning and development. My
main ache here is to literally move with and experience these ten-
sions. We must move our hearts and bodies on all the streets we
share so we can more naturally face what is harming all of us and
cocreate equitable solutions.

HOW I ROLL

Garrett Brumfield is a cherished friend of mine. His motivational movement, Overcome Yours, is deeply needed in this time. He has been a significant source of wisdom for me around the heart of this theme, and he brings immeasurable joy to everyone he encounters.

As a person with a lifelong disability, cerebral palsy, movement has been difficult yet vital to my existence from day one. Early on, countless hours were spent in surgery and physical therapy trying to improve my movement, yet the way I move has still changed over time. Throughout my elementary and middle school years I often walked unassisted or with crutches, and even played recreation basketball on a typical team without any supports. Despite moving at a much slower pace than my teammates, that is when I first unknowingly became an inspiration. I still remember having an in-game play named after me, newspaper articles written about me, and receiving the honor of "Young Hero of the Year" from my home state of Virginia in 2002.

Despite the recognition, I did not feel like a hero. Heroes are those who save lives, not those who simply live life differently due to a disability or other unavoidable circumstance. This realization led me to begin hiding my disability in hopes of people seeing me as a normal person and not simply an inspiration. At the beginning of high school, I stopped wearing leg braces and going to physical therapy and opted to get rid of my paid supports by using a mobility scooter. I changed, again, the way I moved to help make me feel more independent and "normal."

Now at the age of thirty-one, I continue to move mostly by way of my mobility scooter, but I have a much better understanding and acceptance of my disability, my body, and the way it moves best. I also know that if I remain too sedentary, my body gets stiff and sore.

Along with my own self improvements and acceptance, it has been my goal of educating, empowering, and advocating alongside others with disabilities as they too strive for equity, inclusion, and independence. This has led me to partner with many organizations on initiatives to improve areas of education, employment, and health care for people with disabilities. However, the area of advocacy that I am most passionate about improving is the built environment. I have heard it said that the area of advocacy that someone will have the most passion for is that which affects them most. That is indeed true for me as the built environment has long been my biggest nemesis. Whether it be when ramps, curb cuts, and elevators are nonexistent or waiting days for sidewalks to be shoveled after a snow, all of this presents unnecessary challenges for me and others who have impairments—be they from limited mobility, vision, or hearing. But these issues can also affect parents with strollers as well.

Sure, we need universal design, but first we need understanding from those movers and decision-makers who do not face these same challenges. We need more awareness for those of us who move differently. Drivers of vehicles need to slow down and always remain alert for pedestrians so we can cut down on injuries and fatalities. The "Every Corner is a Crosswalk" and "No Need to Speed" campaigns that I have recently been a part of with my local bike-pedestrian commission are about just that: raising awareness. Pedestrians with disabilities are often lower to the ground and are at much higher risk of not being seen by drivers.

I know life gets busy, but everyone can do their part in creating change by slowing down and increasing your understanding related to what others go through, regardless of whether you live life at sixty miles per hour going down a highway, walk at three miles per hour, or roll at five miles per hour like I do. We must respect each other by first accepting that we all move and live differently, and there is nothing at all wrong with that.

WAKING UP: A HUMAN RIGHT

It took many years of vomiting up all the filth I'd been taught about myself, and half-believed, before I was able to walk on the Earth as though I had a right to be here.

—JAMES BALDWIN (1988)

I have a right to move the way I am made to.

I have a right to feel safe, comfortable, and connected to my surroundings.

I have a right to nourish my cells, neurons, and breath with healthy movement.

I have a right to process emotion, stress, and trauma the way I am made to.

I have a right to be connected to the natural world.

I have a right to physically move next to loved ones, neighbors, strangers, and friends.

Black families and children have a right to feel just as safe on public streets as white families and children.

Indigenous families and children have a right to feel just as safe on public streets as white families and children.

People with disabilities have a right to walk or roll safely and comfortably on public streets.

Transgender people, nonbinary people, and all nonconforming people have a right to walk or roll safely on public streets.

Women have a right to walk or roll safely and comfortably on public streets.

We, the beloved human story, representing all races, gender identities, sexual orientations, abilities, ages, and backgrounds, *have a right* to safely move by foot or on a wheelchair on all public streets.

Take a deep breath and reread these lines. Read them slowly and more fully, perhaps out loud. If you influence transportation decisions in your community or city, write them down and read them before your next meeting, or all of your meetings, as a collective.

DEDICATED PRACTICE

Take some time to move with the practice below. Do you know the Indigenous tribal lands you are walking or rolling on? Learn from and honor them as you move. Listen to your body. Honor your needs. Honor the lived reality of all who walk or use a wheelchair as their primary form around you. Honor what will work for you, especially depending on your ability, community, and context. No rules. Only invitation.

Felt Knowledge

Our crisis around moving the way we are made becomes more urgent and real when we actually bring our bodies into the tension, no matter whether rural, suburban, or urban.

Some of the greatest gaps facing public agencies are staff shortages, fixed budgets, and cross-department collaboration, especially when related to the full practical trip. Someone walking or rolling from point A to point B might interact with a variety of public and private systems. This means change is slow, disconnected, and often nonexistent. If we could steward more cross-department, cross-agency walking and rolling events in areas that are harmful for pedestrians and those in wheelchairs, I trust we would see more focused improvements in the places that need it the most. Get to know these groups. Inspire them to walk or roll on the very networks they are positioned to serve.

Grounding: I invite you to pause before moving with this practice. Take a few deep breaths with the following frames:

In breath: "I have a right to feel safe in my body."

Out breath: "I have a right to be here."

In breath: "I have a right to feel safe in my body."

Out breath: "I have a right to move the way I am made to."

Add your own words and expressions to this breathing exercise and repeat as often as you want to help ground your body, heart, and intention.

If Walking, Rolling and Riding Public Transit Is Your Primary Form of Transportation: Try to protect whatever extra time you can to document and honor your lived experience by making it more public. Notice what is hard, stressful, chaotic, and challenging, both in your body and in your environment. Notice when your transportation experience is influencing your emotions and mental health. Notice when your transportation experience leaves you out of important gatherings, connections, and appointments. Take photos and record video or audio. Write a story or reflection and see if a local paper or community organization will publish it or feature it. Carry a pocket journal to make sketches or write poetry. Make connections with folks who work to maintain and care for your transportation experience. Seek out local advocacy groups for sharing your stories, art, and reflections.

If Driving Is Your Primary Form of Transportation:

Planning and Prep: Protect time on your next walk or roll to intentionally witness, experience, and absorb what pedestrians, families, people with disabilities, children, and more face on a daily basis related to the environments surrounding your home, workplace, or community. Study where post offices, bus stops, recreation centers, schools, grocery stores, and libraries are in your community. Notice what access is like to these practical destinations. Are mixed-income residential housing, public housing, or senior living communities nearby? How might people navigate their surroundings or arrive to their destinations if they aren't driving? To dive in deeper, craft your walk or roll around your own practical trips. Replace everyday trips to the doctor, grocery store, post office, school, workplace, or library with as much human-powered transportation as you are able. No cars. For this practice, try to avoid ride-shares. See the transit adaptation at the end if you want to narrow your focus. Protect time to reflect on these experiences: What did you learn? How difficult was it? Who did you witness, connect with, and learn from? What surprised you? Would you be willing to organize a walk or roll with decision-makers, inviting them into what you have learned and experienced?

Time: This is completely dependent on your pace and if you are weaving in your own practical trips. If moving in this way is new for you, give yourself plenty of extra time. If you are not doing a loop, be sure to build in enough time to walk or roll back. Research public transit routes near you and perhaps have a couple of friends to dial in case you need additional options for getting back.

Location: As already mentioned, do your best to make your location based on personal (or popular) practical trips. Housing or residential areas to grocery, school, library, human services, bus stops, using commercial corridors, state highways or arterial roadways, and roads that have popular bus routes.

Safety: Be sure to walk opposite to car traffic if you find yourself on a busy commercial roadway with no walking facilities. Consider wearing reflective or bright clothing so that you are easily seen. Avoid being on the phone, and try to not have music or earbuds in on high-traffic sections so you can be extra attentive to your safety and surroundings. If you stop to take a photo, to read your checklist, or to record your experience, be sure you are off somewhere away from being directly next to automobile traffic.

Adaptations

Public Transit: Center your focus on local bus stops and various transit locations. What are they like? Are they safe, comfortable, and accessible? Why or why not? Are there public restrooms? Next, take the bus, train, shuttle, or any other form of public transportation yourself. I highly recommend using whatever system is in place to get to and from a specific practical destination: home to work, home to store, home to post office. Can't find a stop? Can't connect to a service or system? Is it easy to find information on what systems exist? All of this is extremely helpful information related to equity, access, public health, isolation, and connection. Notice transit waiting times. Notice flexibility and frequency of times. Notice if it is easy to understand fares, schedules, and payment options. Notice if there are other languages represented online and on schedule boards. Notice accessibility and safety at the stop itself. Notice when you need to use the restroom. Notice when you are feeling hungry or thirsty. How could these systems be improved to honor and prioritize those who depend on them?

Facing the Elements: Intentionally walk or roll in the rain, with snow and ice, in the heat of the day, in rush-hour traffic, and along popular corridors at night. Be as safe and as comfortable as you can with a raincoat, umbrella, waterproof shoes, bright clothing, flashing lights, or reflectors. You might also want to do this with a friend or peer, especially if you are unfamiliar with an area. Notice what choices people have or don't have when it comes to getting away from the heavy rain, alternate routes with snow and ice obstacles, using the restroom, and shade from a blistering sun.

4

WALKING AS EARTH CARE

LAND RIGHTS, ACEQUIAS, AND YOUTH

"The People's Ditch was hand-dug by my ancestors and is the life-line for this community," shared one of our youth walking leaders to a public group of participants. As we listen, the calming flow of acequia water gracefully rushes next to us. Our walk starts at what is called the People's Ditch on the southside of town in San Luis, Colorado. As we gather under friendly cottonwood canopies, a cool breeze whispers through the leaves. Slowing down has allowed us to breathe more deeply and be with the awe of the lush valley surrounding us.

It is a Saturday, and entire families are out working in the fields or tending to their animals. It is amazing to see people who have come from nearby towns or as far as distant cities walking next to these incredible young people. I am filled with life as I slowly walk in the back, observing and taking it all in. They exchange questions, share stories, and drink in the surroundings of a landscape that has fought hard to avoid ongoing predatory development. This area is only a fifteen- to twenty-minute drive to the New Mexico border, and most of the people who call it home carry a one-of-a-kind language they refer to as San Luis Valley Spanish. It is a unique blend of Spanish influenced by Spain and Mexico, mixed Indigenous languages, and English. Most of the people here are mixed Latino, Chicano, Hispanic, and Indigenous, specifically Ute, Jicarilla Apache, Kiowa, Navajo, and Comanche.

We are being guided by an amazing team of young people who are a part of a small cohort of walking leaders across the San Luis Valley. They have been trained and supported by local historians, community leaders, community organizations, and Walk2Connect to host public heritage and land stewardship walks for the summer season.

We stop as we make our way out of the town of San Luis. The youth leaders point first to the large grassy area surrounding the People's Ditch. They refer to their water ditches as acequias. This large, 633-acre area is one of two remaining commons, belonging to the people, in the country. It is used primarily for grazing cattle and horses five months of the year. There are so many shades of green. The movement and air are grounded and quiet. We continue walking south along this rural road. We pass old adobes, ranches, and some of the oldest homesteads in the country. We are embarking on a ten-mile walking journey from the town of San Luis to and through the Culebra Basin villages of San Pedro, Chama, Los Fuertas, San Pablo, and San Francisco (El Rito).

Neighbors wave and look at our youth-guided group with curiosity. Once they see that some of their own are leading the way, they come out to greet us or stop in the road while driving by to learn more. Our mobile portable toilet on a trailer is also a creaky, jumbly sight to behold as it follows along. We take breaks, eat, and celebrate our movement in each of the villages.

One of my favorite outcomes of longer-distance group walks is that it would be odd or abnormal to encourage sitting, lying down, and rolling around on the ground at the start of our walk.

By lunchtime, we are all in the grass. Some of us are dunking our heads in the nearby acequia to cool off. Some of us are leaning against the cool trunk of a cottonwood. Some of us have feet and legs raised on the fence with backs flat on the dirt. In a small amount of time our connection to the Earth is entirely more intimate than what it was when we were all in cars, inside of walls, or scrolling on screens.

As we get a little farther along, one of the youth leaders stops us. "Those mountains over there. They are the Sangre de Cristo Mountains. They are what our people refer to as La Sierra. They are the sacred mountains that we have depended on for generations. These mountains, all eighty thousand acres of them, and our rights to access them are a part of one of the largest land-grant fights in the country, *Lobato* v. *Taylor*. Having gone through multiple private landowners, the people of our community, especially the heirs of the 1844 Sangre de Cristo Land Grant, have had to fight the courts for over forty years to protect just some of our most basic rights related to using trees for wood and fire, grazing our animals, hunting, and recreating. In 2018, and with the help of an amazing team of pro bono attorneys, we officially won our case in front of the Colorado Supreme Court to lock in some of these rights in perpetuity. We have many fights ahead, but now every family who manages land and is related to a family heir can have a key to open all of the gates to access our mountains."

We continue moving. The valley is wide and spacious. The calmness of the air holds each of us and all that swirls after hearing this important story. Each tree, each flower, each drop of water, and each stone has more to say. We are inspired by our young leaders who grew up playing and connecting to these mountains. We honor what they are teaching us and wrestle with big questions related to land ownership and injustice.

We sit in the grass and rest. We all run toward the sound of flowing water to cool off along our route. We thank the trees for their shade, play and rest on rocks, chase butterflies, and peer into the color and magic of wildflowers. We allow the bigness of the sky and the wisdom of clouds to inspire us. We sing and dance on spacious dirt roads that seem to have no end in sight.

We finally arrive after a long and wondrous day into the small village of San Francisco that sits at the base of Culebra Peak. This is the home of my dear friends Junita and Jose Martinez. It is one of my most cherished places. They are like family to me. The trees are full of memories, dreams, prayers, and stories. As we gather after our walk, we listen to stories and wisdom shared by Shirley Romero Otero, who is known all over the country for her role in the land grant fight. Shirley inspires me to no end and has given so much of her life to weave radical Earth protection into the hearts of young people.

El agua es vida (Water is Life) is printed in bold blue letters on a sticker that was gifted to me by Junita shortly after our first summer youth-guided walks. This phrase, its deep interconnected invitation, and the experiences walking with these young people go with me everywhere. Walking as Earth care is bold, playful, wondrous, devastating, and urgent. When we walk with each other, the needs of our deep hearts and the needs of the planet become ever-present. How does this story inspire you to move and connect to all the lineages, tribes, fields, dirt roads, mountains, streams, beaches, and valleys around you?

INTEGRATION PRACTICE:
TRACING AND NURTURING WATERSHEDS

Start by doing some research on various watersheds (creeks, rivers, streams, ditches, canals) near you. Study their shape, direction, and pattern. Find ways to get to them. Draw a map to visualize how they flow around you. Look up their source (headwaters). Look up where they end (the mouth). I have spent more days than I can count walking alongside flowing water. There is something so important that happens when we increase our proximity to water. Perhaps because our bodies are mostly made of water? Start with the nearest park, river walkway, creek path, greenway, or conservation area where access is allowed. As you move along various streams, learn to identify native plants and trees, local birds, bee species, and critter habitats. Open your heart toward all the animals and groups of people who have depended on these waterways for centuries. You might also spend some time learning about who currently uses these water systems for crops, irrigation, disposal, pollution, and waste. As you protect more time to move alongside flowing water, you will more naturally pay attention to what your water habitats need and what you and your community can do to help them thrive.

I Am of this World

NATURE PROXIMITY

I deeply believe that the closer we are to nature, the more human we become. When I say "human," I am not talking about humans at the center, but the more natural, nonlinear, and circular alignment between our existence and that of nature. We awaken to the humbling notion that *we are nature* and not separate from it. When I say "closer," I am not only speaking of physical proximity, but emotional, mental, and spiritual proximity as well. If we are physically close to nature, but not also connecting our inner purpose, truths, and worthiness with it as well, then it is all too easy for us to extract it, use it, and see it only as a commodity.

Our journey to care for the soul of nature requires the journey to care for our own. I believe the more we can slow down to humbly move into communion with the sky, ground, and trees, the more we can humbly move with all that moves inside us. This intimate invitation requires constant letting go and constant openness to receive what nature longs to reveal.

We more naturally want to help keep our waterways clean because we are nourished and sustained by their flowing presence.

We make more room to move with the wisdom of water.

We make more room to care for and protect our water.

We more naturally want trees and forests to thrive because we honor our own breath and all created life.

We make more room to move with the wisdom of trees.

We make more room to care for and protect our trees.

We more naturally pay attention to what we eat because we witness what animals and ecosystems go through when treated as commodities.

We make more room to move with the wisdom of cows, birds, bees, and fish.

We make more room to care for and protect cows, birds, bees, and fish.

We more naturally honor the gifts and purpose of fresh air, a warm sun, snowcapped winters, and a clear blue sky.

We make more room to move with the wisdom of the biosphere.

We make more room to care for and protect the biosphere.

THE TREE PEOPLE

The following story is by my cherished friend Arbolista. Her love for, trust in, and dedication to the trees moves with me wherever I go.

> We have so much in common with trees that I consider them family. We're made up of the same things, like energy from the sun and minerals from the Earth. We both need food and water to survive, and we share DNA. They give so much to us, like their wood for warmth, shelter from the elements, and oxygen to breathe.
>
> Years ago, I learned that my Native American ancestors bent trees to guide the way to water, to safe passages across rivers, to good hunting grounds, and to good places to set up their villages. They recognized and acknowledged the trees as living beings, so they asked permission to modify their shape to stand out from the vertical ones. When rations were low and they needed sustenance, they peeled the bark of ponderosa pines. They took some of the cambium layer because it's rich in vitamin C and ground it into a paste. They made tea from its needles and cradle boards to carry their babies. Medicine was made from willow bark. *Inipis,* or sweat lodges, were built for their sacred spiritual ceremonies. They didn't waste anything. The importance of the "tree people" was taught to their children so that they knew how to show as much love, respect, and care for the trees as the trees showed to them.
>
> I have walked among the trees on sacred ground where my ancestors lived and loved. It was there that I heard the sounds of the drumming circle, the breath of a flute, and the voice of

an elder guiding me along the right path. I have even witnessed the branches of bushes waving to me, as if to say, "We are grateful to see you!"

My ancestors have always known that trees have healing properties. People today often call it "forest bathing" when going into the forest to sit among the trees and breathe in a chemical called phytoncides. Trees emit this to protect themselves from insects and germs. Many practice it as a form of therapy to lower stress and increase focus.

Trees deserve our respect, and we need to honor them. They hold ancient wisdom that we've disregarded as a society for too long. We've moved away from that connection and have become sick because of it. All that they offer is free. Get close to an old orange ponderosa pine and smell its aroma of vanilla and butterscotch. Exhale the carbon dioxide it converts into oxygen. Offer it a drink of water and it just might communicate its wisdom with you. Speak your prayers to it, if you're so inclined, and it will hold them until the wind picks them up and they're carried to the Creator on the wings of soaring eagles.

INTEGRATION PRACTICE: BREATHING WITH TREES

As you begin your movement, begin to form a new or renewed relationship with the trees that surround you. Get to know them. Visit and revisit them. Notice them in the morning, in the middle of the day, and in the evening. Notice them from different vantage points: far away from different sides, close to the bark and leaves, from inside your home or workplace, looking up under their branches, kneeling to feel and see their roots. Imagine them inviting you to breathe with them. As you notice them, be extra aware of your in-breath and your out-breath. Honor the literal life-giving relationship you share with them—how they receive your carbon dioxide, and you receive their oxygen. Before you move along, allow for a moment of calm gratitude with the tree. Rest your hand on its bark. Lean your shoulders on it. Look up at its canopy. Notice how the branches bend, fold, and twist. Close your connection with gratitude and presence.

WHEN DID IT BREAK?

For those of us who grew up in a consumer-influenced society, there lives a web of moments and experiences, in our own lives and in the lives of those who came before us, where one's intrinsic, intimate, and playful relationship to the planet was severed. Mutual and relational connection to nature became solely or primarily seeing it as a commodity, a container for activity, or a place of retreat.

This "break" in relationship has convinced too many of us that we are not only separate from nature, but that nature is solely for our use. It also invites an important picture around how we care for one another and our more tender selves. How might poor treatment of the planet be connected to our treatment of humanity? In the words of adrienne maree brown:

> The Earth is layer upon layer of all that has existed, remembered by the dirt. It is time to turn capitalism into a fossil, time to turn the soil, turn the horizon together.... Let's all be conduits of the wisdom of this planet. I think any efforts to engage the emergent brilliance of our world will help with this turning, will help with liberating humanity from its current role as a virus Earth should shake off (brown 2017, 49).

Be with these rumbling words. Whether you agree with them or not, I invite you to move with what Adrienne is inviting. Why would she refer to humanity's role like a virus on the Earth? Why might she be inviting us to turn capitalism into a fossil? Instead of putting up walls, I invite you to move with these questions and deeply feel what we need to be paying attention to for our own health and survival, for the health and survival of numerous species in our midst, and for future generations.

Try to name and be with what keeps so many of us from the calming sound of flowing streams, smelling wildflowers, resting with a rising sun, and seeing ourselves in twisting branches. If we were more naturally able to feel sustained and nourished by what is natural, would we still feel the need to find ourselves in, under, and surrounded by so much plastic? As our lives give way to artificial materials and harmful stories of separation from all the ecosystems that make breath, food, and water possible, our detachment and disconnection only gets deeper.

MOVING WITH EYES WIDE OPEN

The following story is by my dear friend and herbalist Monticue Connally of Jiridon Apothecary and A Root Awakening. His vibration in the world inspires me every day.

> When I was young, I wanted to transcend the mundane and enter another world. I wanted to move out of this body and off of this planet into the great mystery to inherit a great power. I would meditate on each chakra for months and months hoping that in some perfect instant my mind would be engulfed in an amazing spiritual fire. I was sure that with practice and patience I'd be in another place surrounded by angelic beings of great wisdom.
>
> I wanted these kinds of experiences, and in my early twenties I started to have them mostly in the form of astral travel adventures. But as amazing as this was, it wasn't enough. I still felt like something was missing.
>
> When I became an herbalist, I found myself in the forest more. I was particularly interested in harvesting wild medicines. One

day while walking down a path in a beautiful meadow, I took a seat and decided to meditate. My meditations were always done with my eyes closed, the way I'd seen it done in books and television as a youth. But as I settled in and pulled my attention inward, something told me to leave them open. I tried to ignore the voice, but it wouldn't go away. It only grew louder. Confused, I allowed my eyes to open. I relaxed and let my mind stay in that meditative place. I noticed the environment around me had shifted slightly in color and that I could distinctly feel the presence of angelic beings.

I sprang to my feet and began to walk with this meditative mental state intact. I smiled and my heart was filled with joy as I realized that in this space, I could clearly sense who these angels were. These angels were the active subtle bodies of the spirits of nature. Various plants in flower, old rocks, and tall trees with big gnarly roots were the angels I had been looking for my entire life, and they'd been here the whole time.

The story in my mind had been telling me to meditate in stillness with my eyes closed only. This is what I was taught to do. Who would have thought that walking with eyes wide open through a forest could be a meditative, angelic adventure? I have been on many walks in the forest since then, and I've carried this lesson with me. The spiritual heart is our best organ of perception and a bridge to our guides, on the inside and the outside.

INTEGRATION PRACTICE:
PLANT RELATING

As you begin your movement, at a park or in your neighborhood, try focusing on what Monticue so beautifully describes as "angelic beings." Start by zeroing in on one specific plant. Go beyond just seeing it. Get closer to it and rest with it. Gaze into its details. Notice

its color. Notice the shape and texture of the leaves. Does it have
flowers or buds? Are there thorns? If you have a notebook or sketchbook, try drawing it. Take a close-up photo. Learn the many names
used to identify it. Is it edible? Does it embody medicinal properties?
What creatures depend on it, use it, and live with it? From there, you
will notice it everywhere you go. Your connection to it, like anything,
will become more whole.

HEARTS AND GUTS

As we invite more time moving with and peering into the details of
fragrant, leafy miracles, let's also keep our role to help care for them
just as close. I could have stacked this entire chapter in statistics on
how harmful ambient air pollution coming from motor vehicles is,
especially when used every day for every trip, for our atmosphere,
crops, sea levels, plants, trees, polar ice caps, and the fragile lungs in
grandmothers and children. I chose not to because I want to avoid
keeping you too long in your mind, thinking, measuring, studying.
I am not interested in convincing you of anything intellectually. I
want you to move with more intention, openness, and creativity. I
want your heart and body to vibrate more honestly and fully.

Heart wisdom can help us fall in love with all that is alive in
nature while also guiding us to empathize with what harms it. Body
or gut wisdom can keep us close to our lived experience. *I know
because I walk or roll in it. I know because I stop to rest by the flowing water. I know because I find love and inspiration in a sunset. I know
because I feel vulnerable walking and sweating on high-speed streets.*

Without heart and gut experiences, the mind all too often
darts around without ground. Thinking and cold reason alone
leaves us off balance. If there is no empathy, exposure, or lived

experience, it is too easy for those who benefit from oppressive systems to stay comfortable and separated from the harm caused by those systems.

Water systems, forests, wild fish populations, and critters are disappearing all around us. Our capacity to nourish and nurture our own species is breaking down. Rainbows, fall leaves, and butterflies still call out to us. Trees and plants still choose to breathe with us. Walking as Earth care is courageous. It is a web of invitations, with humble descent into many waves of risk and discomfort. It is also redeeming and profoundly healing. This blazing, beautiful, chaotic, and costly relationship cries out to each of us.

DEDICATED PRACTICE

Take some time to move with the practice below. Do you know the Indigenous tribal lands you are walking or rolling on? Learn from and honor them as you move. Listen to your body. Honor your needs. Honor the lived reality of all who walk or use a wheelchair as their primary form around you. Honor what will work for you, especially depending on your ability, community, and context. No rules. Only invitation.

Who Must I Become?

Our proximity and connection to the natural world is vital for us to feel and embody a relationship that is mutual and caring. Much like our connections with one another, our relationship to the planet should move toward vulnerability, honesty, healing, listening, dreaming, and unconditional love. Deep inner work to love our own interior landscape is critical to see, love, and respect the landscapes around us more genuinely.

Preparation: Your dedicated walking practice is to make a specific connection to Earth stewardship as you move. Bring the five questions below with you as you walk or roll. You could bring all five and read them first to yourself and then again out loud. You could also bring one question for one walk and make this into a five-part series. Allow each question, as you move, to open, challenge, and inspire your journey.

1. What must I risk, let go of, and seek to deepen my connection to the Earth?

2. Is my unhurried movement helping me to see more naturally and be with nature? If so, what am I seeing or feeling that I wasn't before?

3. How must I live to integrate my personal ideas of Earth care with systemic actions, workplace behaviors, local organizing, education, and change?

4. What costs, fears, challenges, and sacrifices—specifically to comfort, reputation, and likeability—arise as I invite integrated awakening and change?

5. Who must I become to have a more active, felt, and embodied relationship to Earth stewardship?

Grounding: Before you begin your movement, you might kneel and touch the ground or place your hand on a nearby tree. From there, invite the Earth into your breathing. Take several deep breaths. Slow down your mind and open your senses. Invite the Earth to speak to you throughout your experience. Honor that "you are the Earth" and not separate from it.

Movement: As you move with one or all of these questions, you might take notes, draw pictures, record audio, or capture a video. You might also just let them move deeper and deeper into your heart, step by step, roll by roll. Listen, allow, and open. Repeat reading each question aloud. You might read your questions while looking into the details of a tree, or the patterns in the sky, or the crystal flow of nearby water.

As you deepen this practice, revisit that same tree, stone, stream, or nest and go through the questions again. Continue revisiting these elements with these questions again ... and again ... and again. Notice how they look or feel the same and different depending on the time of day or season. Notice any changes in your connection over time.

As you close your walks, I invite you to integrate what you feel and experience into unique actions you can take to more intentionally protect and care for these special connections. What is the quality of the water? Do I know where it comes from and if factories are dumping into it? Do I know what would help this large, mature tree thrive? Why are there no native indigenous plants with wildflowers and bees in this area? Why don't I see bird nests or butterflies? Can I pick up trash on my next walk? Can I bring a neighbor or community leader with me?

Location: Go toward plants, trees, open sky, rushing water, and other various natural elements. If you are in a city, go toward the parks, the tree-lined streets, the flowers, and river or creek areas. If you are limited to concrete-heavy environments, go toward the trees that fight to survive, peer into the sky, and seek the flowers growing out of the cracks of the sidewalk.

Time: Take at least thirty to forty-five minutes. This will allow you to relax more into your body, open your senses, and enrich your capacity to listen and reflect on the gifts and needs of the natural world around you.

Sun, Sky & Stars

humans hearts BEings

...Trees & Branches

how am I connecting?

defined: the way in which two or more go into

Relationship

with...

how am I opening?

Concepts, objects, or people are connected

...Rocks Roots & Soil

Critters & Birds

Storms & Storms

5

WALKING AS RELATIONSHIP

CREATION CALLING

From a distance I saw them noticing my slow-moving frame. Their large heads and necks were facing my direction. They kept their eyes on me for several minutes. I could feel them watching me.

It was day 7 walking a new route I was scouting from Fort Collins to Pueblo along Colorado's front range. It was a mix of residential neighborhoods, historic main streets, river greenways, open-space parks, small highways, trails, and rural dirt roads. I had just made my way out of Larkspur and was slowly moving through thick storybook fog. The mountains in the distance were impossible to see. Large ranches and farms dotted the road in the distance on both sides.

I decided to move down the grassy ditch from the raised roadway toward their fence. They were far enough away to not feel threatened, but close enough to discern whether I was to be trusted. Cars rush past them on this side of the ranch all hours of the day. The sight of a human body slowly walking on the road was out of place. As I approached the fence, I thought they might come up to me. One horse was all white, another was mostly white with large brown patches, and the third was chocolate brown with dark-brown hair. As I stopped and stood by the fence, I called out to them, "Hello-o-o." I saw them looking at each other. "Should we go?"

It was comical to watch.

One didn't budge. "Nope."

One was open. "Sure, I guess; why not."

The other was tossing his head with excitement and delight. "Yes, my gosh, this will be fun!"

They seemed to have decided to let me continue on my way as they stayed huddled together while I called. So, I waved them farewell, and I continued to walk south. This was a large ranch property but would be coming to an end in a few minutes. I remained on their side of the road in case their curiosity got the best of them.

I could still feel their energy. I kept turning my head back, and I saw the brown-and-white painted one jumping around the two who were still undecided. A few moments passed, and the painted one had enough. He started running to catch up with where I was. They were still far away, but the other two eventually dragged along behind him. As they started to move, the slow movers perked up, and all three of them were now running with me at a distance.

It was hilarious, playful, and beautiful.

With all the mist and fog, we were in our own magical world. No ranchers or cars for a good thirty to forty minutes. Just the four of us. They were all moving together, and they eventually passed me and ran ahead toward where the fence ends. They came right up to the edge, and all three of them were waiting. The white one remained mostly uninterested but was curious. The chocolate one was cautious but eager to meet. The painted one was full of excitement and waiting for me to pet his long, beautiful nose. I laughed and teared up.

I stayed with them for several minutes. Lots of eye contact, nose rubs, ear scratches, and wordless vibrations were exchanged. My entire body felt greeted, welcomed, and seen by them. Our playful greeting brought me life. I felt deeply connected to them, even if it was just for a moment. I said goodbye to my new friends. I kept turning my head back as their long faces watched me walk away into the fog.

THE FREE ONE

The gifts that were exchanged between my own unique existence and the unique existence of these incredible horses lives all around us. They saw me. They spoke to me. They felt my presence. I saw them. I spoke to them. I felt their presence. For anyone who has raised animals or moved through life with pets, you may already resonate with this profound connection.

I will never forget stumbling into a local animal shelter in 2009. It was less than a year before setting off on my cross-country walk, and I was discerning the possibility of having a dog join me. For this first visit, I told myself I would not be leaving with a new pet. I was only there to feel it out.

I moved through the hallways watching dogs of all sizes, ages, and shapes. Some were right up on the glass jumping and yelping. Some were too tired to care.

I noticed him right away.

He was bored and uninterested in trying to impress anyone. His fur was all knotted up and covered in dirt, and they gave him the name Alfalfa. The sticker on the wall said he was a blue heeler, cattle dog, and husky mix. When I walked by the first time, I felt drawn to him, but committed to my agreement. He didn't stop looking at me, but he also didn't respond like some of the others. I moved along, farther down the hallway.

That face. Those eyes. His goofy lopped ear. That curly tail. He was quite the misfit. I couldn't stop thinking about him.

I turned back. I looked over at him again, and his eyes didn't leave mine. He didn't get up and jump around, but something was already happening between us. I can't explain it. I grumbled around my intention not to leave this place with a pet. Five minutes later I was sitting in a small visitation room while the staff got him ready.

As soon as the door opened, he came running up to me. He was unconditional love erupting. He licked me, pushed into me, and tried to throw his eighty-pound frame onto my lap. He whimpered the whole time. It was within minutes of us meeting that I just knew. We both knew. How do you possibly explain what was happening between us in that small room?

In just twenty minutes, it was clear. He was coming home with me. The staff shared with me that he was found on the I-70 interstate in Denver, and by the look of his fur, had probably been out roaming for days or even weeks.

I will never forget the day my adopted godmother Carol and I went to pick him up. It was the beginning of a relationship that I would cherish with everything I had. I knew that the first year of his life was mostly in crates, cages, and walls. I wanted his name to have meaning. I wanted his name to honor his journey and honor the journey we would share together. I named him Kanoa, which is Hawaiian for "the free one."

My connection to Kanoa has endlessly shaped my ideas and understandings of "relationship." He watches my every move. He knows when I'm not well. I know when he's not well. We have a precious communication system that mostly involves muffled barks and grunts. We have walked thousands and thousands of miles together. When I kiss him on the forehead and rest my cheeks on his, I feel us touching realms far beyond this one.

Having Kanoa at my side on my cross-country walk was one of the greatest gifts of my life. We walked, side by side, into wondrous places of freedom and healing. We both looked out for each other, and we shared everything. We ran, jumped, napped, ate, howled, and sweated our way across hundreds of landscapes. He is still unconditional love erupting.

GOING INTO RELATIONSHIP WITH ...

How might you move more intentionally into the energy, air, or aura that moves and lives between you and another life form? What in your life helps you daily experience this great connection between you and another human being, perched birds, colorful plants, crawling caterpillars, rushing rivers, slowly swimming ducks, and curious cows? Going *into relationship with* asks us to expand our eyes and hearts to what arises—wisdom, information, energy—as two life forces come together, whether for a moment, for weeks, or for a lifetime. Relationship in this context stretches far beyond human-centric constructs of just romantic partners, biological family, chosen family, or friends. For this invitation, I am speaking of a quality of connection that lives in between two or more life forms. According to one of my friends and teachers, Franciscan Richard Rohr:

> The mystics would say whenever you stand apart and objec-
> tify anything, you stop knowing it. You have to love, respect,
> and enter into relationship with what you desire to know.
> Then the mirroring goes back and forth, subject to sub-
> ject, center to center, love to love. Then the loving becomes
> its own kind of knowing. This is knowing by participation
> (Rohr 2017).

Try to really feel this invitation by slowly rereading Richard's poetic words again. Allow the questions. Allow the doubt. Allow more room for curiosity and wonder. Allow them to guide you into more unexplored or nuanced connection with everyone and everything that is alive around you. What would life be like if you spent more time honoring the actual air and breath living between you and other living organisms? What might be more colorful in your life if you spent more time seeking the complex spaces between your particular life story and that of another?

INTEGRATION PRACTICE:
NATURE SEES ME

Begin with a few mindful breaths. Breathing deeply in: I am seen by the natural world around me. Breathing slowly out: I see and honor the natural world around me. Repeat a few times. Begin to slowly move. Be extra mindful of things that you might normally rush past. When you notice a flower, a stick, a rock, a bird, a critter, or a tree branch catching your attention, try to follow the invitation. Humbly move physically or energetically toward it. With openness and curiosity, allow and invite the notion that the trees, birds, and streams are drawing you closer to them. Move with an awareness that you are worthy of being fully seen by the natural world around you. Move with an awareness that relationship is reciprocal and that there is a cosmic, wondrous exchange happening between you and what is alive near you. Try not to understand it. Feel your heart opening toward it. Allow the tree to see you. Allow wildflowers to call you in. You might offer these words to the tree, bird, or stone: "I invite you to visit and see my longings, dreams, and secrets. I trust you with my wounds, fears, and experiences." I invite you to visit the same tree, bird, stream, or stone again, and again. Try to repeat the breathing practice above and release what might be blocking this always available relationship.

nature sees me

WHAT'S BLOCKING THE FLOW?

Thich Nhat Hanh (2018) writes:

> We are not the same. We are not different.... You are life without boundaries.... We inter-are. We inter-are with our ancestors, our descendants, and the whole cosmos.... We are interconnected with all life, and we are always in transformation.

I am filled with wonder and spaciousness as I read this beautiful quote. I am also filled with heartbreak, and often rage, around all that is at work to close, twist, block, or shrink the essence of "inter-are" living in and around us. How can we possibly live this out when most systems and behaviors around us inflate our differences while simultaneously welding us to those who think, look, and consume like us? In addition to this, consider everything that isolates us from activity that would more naturally open us up: physical walls, parking lots, corporate consumption, social media, highways, and automobiles themselves.

What will it take for us to disrupt and detangle from what works so hard to tear up tender and complex relationships? Are you willing and able to prioritize more unhurried movement to nurture and tend to the wide variety of relationships around you? I love the idea of "relational flow." When I speak it or read it, I immediately hear and feel the flowing Arkansas River in Colorado that I have sat next to for hundreds of hours. I think about the juniper trees that twist, shed, and reach in a thousand different ways for more nourishment. I think about calm sunsets as they invite me to rest an often-racing heart and mind. I think about how good it feels to move with, walking or rolling, someone I haven't seen or connected to in a while.

I invite you to close your eyes and take a moment to be with ideas of movement and relational flow. As you lean into your imagination, what begins to show up for you? What are your surroundings like? What animals, plants, or waterways are near you? Who might be moving next to you? Are you experiencing any blocks? This will be different for all of us. Be with this experience, however simple or complex. Consider writing or drawing some of what you see and some of what might be blocking you on a piece of paper.

I now invite you to take notice of the physical environments you spend a significant amount of time in. Invite relational flow into your awareness. Are you inside artificial buildings with mostly 90-degree walls and manufactured materials? How much time do you spend idling in or moving at thirty- to sixty-mile-per-hour speeds in a metal automobile? How much time do you spend in front of screens? How much pavement or concrete is around you? How often are your day-to-day tasks, relationships, and worldviews shaped within these artificial environments?

Why do I say artificial? Invite the following questions for each of the environments you've pictured:

- How do these spaces, interiors, structures, and materials flow back into me?

- How do they guide, ground, and nourish me?

- Do I know who made them?

- Do I know where the materials came from?

- Are the materials pure and unique, or have they been standardized and manufactured?

If the walls are mud and molded by the hands of your grandparents or your village, perhaps they do flow back into you. If the chairs and couches are hand-carved and covered with blankets woven by your mother and her sisters, perhaps they flow back into you. If you used more manufactured materials, but you built or made your space with your own hands, time, care, and attention, perhaps they flow back into you.

Filling life with artificial shelters, toys, buildings, and objects is not just normal, it is revered. Having more stuff, regardless of what it is, who made it, or how it got here, has been wired in our minds and hearts as unquestionably successful and fulfilling. We need more authentic and genuine connection. We need more unscheduled moments with the gifts and mysteries of nature. We need more humble movement tending to the spaces between my complex experiences and yours.

INTEGRATION PRACTICE: SOMATIC LISTENING

Start this practice with several deep breaths and try placing your hands around your gut area. Before you begin, slowly speak the following intentions: "I invite body-based, rhythmic vibration. I invite relational flow to enter the pores of my skin. I invite mystery and nuance. I invite learning and connection beyond the realm of words." As you begin to move, try not to overthink. Steer your attention on your stomach, intuition, heart, skin, and senses as they relate and interact with your surroundings. Imagine all your hair follicles as unique ears, each with its own capacity to listen and absorb wisdom. Notice and feel your feet. Notice and feel your hips. Notice and feel your arms, shoulders, and hands. Honor them. Stretch them. What are they saying? What might the wind and flowing water be communicating to them or through them? What is being exchanged between your skin, heart, and feet and the roots, soil, and trees? Move with these aches and invitations. Try to keep your connection focused on your body as much as you can. Close this movement practice with deep breaths and calm gratitude.

LOVED ONES: MOVING MIRRORS

Who are the people in your life that you spend the most time with? Who are the people in your life that you love, respect, and relate to the most? Who are the people that represent living, breathing mirrors that send affection, care, and even conflict in your direction? Who in your life has had the gift of your uninterrupted gaze? These complex connections, whether family, friends, or romantic partners, are precious stories that hold some of our deepest fears, dreams, memories, and even pain.

As we invite unhurried movement into every fiber of this book, it is especially important for me to name how walking or rolling can profoundly nurture these cosmic connections. If we avoid bringing more tender attention and intention into our most sacred relationships, how do we imagine having the capacity or willingness to do so with animals, trees, and others? While it might feel terrifying or even awkward, how can you curate more intentional movement as a way of processing, sharing, listening, and affirming your journey of growing and coexisting together? Maybe there is no intention. Maybe it is just *being* in motion together, allowing movement, presence, and a miraculous world to surprise you along the way.

Walking as relationship asks us to tend to, risk for, and deeply see all that is mirroring life, aliveness, and existence back to us. The unique connections and vibrations between you and your loved ones, between you and all created life around you, are worthy of care and creative movement. Give it time. Walking and rolling with more openness and intention will take time.

Our wounds and our grief ache to be seen and witnessed by the gifts of a flowing stream. Our dreams and our joy ache to be seen and witnessed by the colors of a sunset. Our coexistence aches for us to more genuinely live as nonthreatening participants with all of creation. Inviting and seeking more relationship and connection on a walk or roll is a profound and precious act in this time.

DEDICATED PRACTICE

Take some time to move with the practice below. Do you know the Indigenous tribal lands you are walking or rolling on? Learn from and honor them as you move. Listen to your body. Honor your needs. Honor the lived reality of all who walk or use a wheelchair as their primary form around you. Honor what will work for you, especially depending on your ability, community, and context. No rules. Only invitation.

―――――――――― **Spaces Between** ――――――――――

Grounding: Take some time to pause and breathe deeply. Imagine your lungs expanding toward the many relationships you are about to encounter. Honor your experiences. Honor where you are in this moment. Honor what is good and what is hard. Close this time of grounding by looking up at the sky, inviting openness to be with all that wants to see you and move with you.

Movement: As you begin to move, pay extra attention to what energetically exists between you and the oak tree, between you and the flowing stream, between you and the people, and between you and the small bird. This might require several brief pauses in your movement. This will require time and slowing down. You aren't trying to solve anything, and you aren't trying to only capture concrete audible and visual communication. Open toward what is vibrationally happening between you and your connection. Might there be other forms of communication taking place? Is there something happening in your heart? Do you feel pulled or called to move closer? Are there millions of unseen particles radiating from your aura that are caught and absorbed between you and nearby plants, people, and critters? We don't need to answer this. Notice it. Imagine it. Be spacious and open. Try also to notice objects that are more manufactured and artificial as you move. Is it harder to make this connection? Keep tuning your senses to all that exists around you. When or if audible or visual communication takes place, notice how it feels and how your added intention impacts your level of shared connection.

Time: Devote at least twenty to thirty minutes. Consider this practice at various times of the day: once in the early morning, once in the middle of the day, and once in the evening. Notice the variety of relationships during different times of day. Consider different lengths for each time you go out. This can also be a great practice for taking with you on longer half-day, full-day, or multiday walking experiences.

Location: Try any and all. Try mixing it up by doing this practice in a park, in an urban setting, in your neighborhood, in a marketplace or commercial area, or along a stream or river. Notice different relational connections as you change locations.

Pair: After you connect to this practice solo, consider trying it with a loved one, partner, friend, or colleague. Invite your partner to share in the grounding practice together. From there, you both can read and move together, inviting the guidance alongside your collective movement. You can also split up and take the guidance with you separately to then come back and share or reflect on your unique individual experiences and connections. Groups could easily flow into this practice in similar ways as pairs. For groups, I would suggest grounding together, splitting off, and closing and reflecting together.

...let us walk it out together
...let us howl at the moon together
...let us tremble and heal together

6

WALKING AS VULNERABILITY

THE SECRET

We started walking. She was anxious. I was anxious. We turned the first corner, and she was eager to know what was going on.

At the time, my mother lived in a suburban Georgia neighborhood with curvy roads, thick forest, churches, strip malls, schools, and drive-throughs. There were limited public parks or trails nearby, so we settled for neighborhood streets and leaving right from her front door. I had just come for a visit after returning from living in Ireland for a year. This was two and a half years before my cross-country walk, but my body knew it wanted to walk with her before too many words were spoken.

I avoided saying anything at the start. She continued asking questions, and it was clear that she wanted me to start speaking right away. It made it hard, but I understood. For much of my upbringing, choosing to go into tension or conflict outside of eruption or suppression was simply nonexistent.

"Can we just walk for just a few more minutes before I say anything?" I asked. She was reluctant but gave way to it. I took a deep breath.

I felt like I was going to get sick.

Intestines twisting.

A hot steamy pile.

Right there on the pavement.

I also felt my feet on the Earth. I asked for guidance from any tree, spirit, cloud, or god who would listen. In those last few wordless minutes, I found a glimpse of harmony with the sky, the fresh air, and the tall branches. I invited them in. I craved for them to help me hold this.

Vulnerability isn't easy.

"Mom," I said.

"Ever since seventh grade ..." I continued.

Something so deep, so confusing, and so loud boiled inside me since seventh grade. I suppressed it, I feared it, I didn't understand it, and I was often controlled by it. It was a private and horribly lonely place. I kept it hidden from everyone, and when I could, which was most days, I kept it hidden from myself. It was the secret no one would ever know.

As a growing teenager, living in the suburbs did not help. Most of the houses looked the same, neighborhood layouts were developed by Wall Street and ideas of false security, watering and cutting grass was the primary relationship to nature, and car- and garage-centric behavior made it all too easy to stay isolated and disconnected.

There were too many situational excuses, distractions, and justifications to remain completely disconnected from what was actually going on inside me, what was actually going on inside of my family and neighbors, and what was aching for attention beyond covenant-controlled gates. For my life and for this body, it was toxic and crushing. It only added to the storm brewing inside.

My mom and I were still walking.

Deep breaths.

Deep breaths.

Deep breaths.

"Oh, Mom. Ever since seventh grade, I've been hiding something from you and from everyone. I have been afraid of it. I have feared it. I didn't, and in so many ways, still don't understand it.

"I didn't have words for it until the last couple of years, and up to the beginning of this summer in Ireland, I had no plans for allowing anyone, absolutely anyone into it.

"The universe had different plans," I continued.

I still remember the details of many sleepless nights when the clouds of sorrow would move in. There was a haunting voice that would speak of self-hatred, lack of worth, and death. "If people knew who you really were ... if they knew what was really going on ... they wouldn't want to be around you ... they couldn't possibly love you," the voices whispered over and over. The voices were like claws, ripping and tearing up any sense of belonging.

I allowed them to sink in. I believed them. I was balancing on a thin rope. Having practices that I could lean on, depending on safe and open people, or trusting nature to help hold some of the pain felt nonexistent. Depth was to be avoided. God and spirituality were almighty, narrow, and exclusive. Nature was off-limits for someone so weak and insecure. There were many nights where I would cry, moan, and grab the floor to keep trying, to keep feeling.

We were still slowly moving.

I faced my mom.

"I almost took my own life two months ago. I stood at the edge of a busy and ..."

Sigh.

Sadness.

Shame.

Head down.

My own tears started to fall.

We kept moving.

Her face and posture started to weaken.

We stopped and she turned toward me.

Her tears started to flow.

"Honey, tell me.

"Please trust me.

"You can tell me anything.

"I will love you no matter what.

"You know this."

More tears.

I motioned us to keep walking.

I'll never forget the fire and fragility of those days. So much inner trembling. As my time in Ireland began to wind down, I knew that I wanted to return home and spend a month with my father and a month with my mother, inviting them all the way in.

All the way. No more lies, no more fronts, and no more toxic turmoil. Vulnerability burst through my glass ceiling that summer. Everything I tried to hold together was now left in pieces on this mysterious floor. It is different now. I move in new skin. I feel vulnerability in new ways. It isn't necessarily comfortable, but it is different.

My mother.

I knew her heart and her deep love for me. It is why I could no longer hide this from her. What I didn't know was how to talk to her about it. I didn't trust sitting down, and I didn't trust being indoors. The thought of being inside walls and across a table made me feel nauseous. It just seemed we would both be crunched by the rigidity of hard white walls and hard, uncomfortable chairs. I wanted movement. I wanted openness. I wanted nature. I wanted these elements to assist us.

I reflected on the many afternoons where I would grab a stick and slowly walk through the overgrown forest just across the road in Ireland. In those moments, I knew that the walls of the house would feed oppressive and negative thoughts inside me. Getting outside always opened my world. Nature nurtured my steps and always seemed to offer glimpses of light, courage, and color. I knew that we just needed to start walking. That's all I hoped for: our steps, the sun, the trees, and space in between.

I was twenty-four years old and far from having tools, awareness, and practice with this sort of thing. The voices that fed on self-hatred remained close. As I got closer to telling her, the voices got louder and cleverer. "You will ruin her. You will damage all her dreams. You will be responsible for the pain she will carry for the rest of your life. You will send her over her own edge. How dare you. You are selfish, unworthy, hell-bound ..." and so on.

Here it goes.

Screaming on the inside "No" to those toxic false voices.

Breathing.

Breathing.

Breathing.

"Mom, I hate labels. I have never connected to them. And ... ever since seventh grade I have struggled with my sexuality. I am attracted to men. I'm not straight, I'm not bisexual, and I'm not sure I connect with gay. I'm just me."

It all came pouring out. The fears, the longings, the doubts, and all the magician-level orchestrating to keep everyone, including myself, hidden from this truth since the seventh grade.

The conversation went on and on.

Tears flowing.

"Son," she muttered.

More tears.

More steps.

The trees swayed.

I remember looking up at the sky several times.

I remember being in my body, fearing her response but trusting the truth, the integrity, the ground from which it all came.

More steps.

"How long have you been struggling?

"Why didn't you tell me before?

"It's all so confusing.

"I don't have any context for this.

"I don't know anyone who is gay."

I didn't butt in. I didn't answer her questions right away. Our patient movement and the way of nature calmly gave way to my ability to just allow whatever needed to spill out. We both needed room.

The art of this sacred pace allowed for all of the broken words to find wider and more open ground. They floated in the air, and they didn't as easily, at least for us, cling to defensive or judgmental responses. They were more like utterings and attempts to move with what was just ... real. The actual words themselves didn't carry as much weight as the physical, motion-held movement of my mother still at my side.

She stopped and collected her tears. She grabbed me by the shoulders.

Sniffling, scrunched, broken ...

"I love you, son. No matter what. Know this."

She stopped again. Elbows bent, combing back her hair, and continuing to wipe her tears.

Looking at me so deep in my eyes ...

"Do you hear me?

"No matter what. I love you."

We hugged a big deep hug and continued moving together.

We didn't have answers.

We didn't have a plan.

We walked in silence for several minutes.

I was far from healed and content.

She was far from healed and content.

What I knew, what she knew ... perhaps without knowing it fully:

She didn't and wasn't going to abandon me.

She loved me and I loved her.

She trusted me, and I trusted her.

The trees were still with us.

The sky was still with us.

The ground was still under our feet.

"I love you, Mom. I don't have all the answers. I don't know what's ahead. But having you here, having this out in the open, and having you loving me through it, makes all the difference in the world."

NURTURING WOUNDS AND PROJECTING PAIN

Be with the essence and complexity of our theme for a moment. Breathe with my story moving alongside my mother and honor where and how it meets you in your unique life experience.

Vulnerability shows up in many forms and is so beyond unique for each of us. Perhaps it is a fiery hole in your gut or a terrifying emotional void. Perhaps it is a mixture of smaller or larger eruptions—anger or sadness—bursting from immediate or long-held experiences of embarrassment, shame, fear, or discomfort. Perhaps it is the way you feel when walking or rolling out in the middle of a busy high-speed roadway to get to the other side. Perhaps it is the way your skin tingles when peering over a bridge or cliff. Maybe it touches all of these or resembles something else entirely.

For many, vulnerability isn't necessarily chosen or intentionally invited. Experiences of vulnerability can often be outright destructive, disorienting, and life-altering. My intention for this theme is not about directly choosing the discomfort of vulnerability itself. It is specifically inviting unhurried movement as a way of tending to the wisdom that lives underneath, around, and through it. More soulful words from my friend, Richard Rohr:

> Did you ever imagine that what we call "vulnerability" might just be the key to ongoing growth? In my experience, healthily vulnerable people use every occasion to expand, change, and grow. Yet it is a risky position to live undefended, in a kind of

constant openness to the other—because it would mean others could sometimes actually wound you (from *vulnus,* "wound"). But only if we choose to take this risk do we also allow the exact opposite possibility: the other might also gift you, free you, and even love you (Rohr 2016, 57).

While so many instances between LGBTQIA2S+ children and their parents never end up how my story did, how we shape spaces and environments for inviting and tending to vulnerability is deeply important. Who or what catches us, sees us, and mirrors back to us love, patience, and acceptance in the midst of our many wounds? Do we feel safe and brave to be vulnerable in our work environments? In our families? In our friend circles? In public? In ourselves?

If we don't have practices or tools around *how* we go into more loving and open time with others and ourselves, then we all too often project what terrifies us. To survive this, we put ourselves and others in limiting, harmful, and unnecessary boxes. Pardon my generalizing here, but if I grow up or have significant life experiences that wound my physical and emotional humanity, and I don't have practices or community to help safely and humbly tend to them, I will ultimately pass it on to others and to the planet. If we are not deeply honest and creative alongside the depths of our own personal and systemic journey to repair, heal, and love, we will continue to feed ongoing destruction.

This invitation isn't about needing to dive directly into and stay in places that are heavy, terrifying, and difficult. What I am aiming to invite is embodied practice that helps us nurture and move with what is really going on inside us. We are made to be *in process.* Our bodies are engineered to help us care for and process trauma and hardship. When we move in this way, our neuro network teams up with our circulatory system, working wonders to massage out tension and evolve our existence. Simply put, the human body needs to move in natural environments to survive emotionally, socially, and physically.

INTEGRATION PRACTICE:
SACRED OBJECTS

As you begin your movement, look for areas where there are natural objects around you: fallen leaves and pinecones, branches, stones. Once you find an area, begin observing the ground. Avoid rushing or overthinking. It might be twenty to thirty minutes or more before you find a spot that speaks to you. From there, if you are able, take a seat or pause and rest. Notice and be with all that is around you. Slowly gather a small collection. You can keep the collection in your hands if you are slowly moving and gathering, or you can create a pile if you are already seated. Once you are seated in the grass, on the sidewalk, or anywhere that calls, begin to place your objects into a pattern or any design that is meaningful to your process. As you observe and place each of the natural objects, try to imagine what the specific stick or leaf or stone could resemble related to your thoughts, aches, and emotions. It might be clear to you, or it might take a while to reveal. Perhaps nothing is coming up. That's okay. Keep returning to what you are creating. Your collection might be in the shape of a swirl, heart, circle, or nothing identifiable. Allow it to be its own unique shape, just as you invite allowing yourself to be your own unique shape. As you place objects, notice texture and details. Be mindful of the textures and details in your life: joy, experiences, dreams, stress, people, hardships. Notice wounds and breaks on the branches, bark, and stones. Invite your own wounds and breaks to surface. Once you feel good about your collection, be with it, listen to it, and allow it to continue speaking to your process. Maybe take a photo or sketch it once you move along. Close with self-compassion and gratitude.

FALSE ARMOR

I think about football helmets in relationship to the actual design of the human brain. The brain floats in water, and every time there is a crash, the brain still crashes against the skull. The surface layers might be somewhat protected, but the deeper inner brain damage is complex and often severe. Now imagine fragile human bodies in automobiles. Sure, we have seat belts and air bags, but we still face the same dilemma. No amount of padding or fancy technology can deny that the fundamental design and system of a fragile human body moving at thirty to seventy miles an hour in a hard metal box is flawed.

In addition to this, what might slowly be happening to our inner emotional, social, environmental, and mental milieu when so many of us spend hours upon hours sitting and speeding through the world inside of hard shells? I have carried these words written by Rebecca Solnit for years:

> Many people nowadays live in a series of interiors ... disconnected from each other. On foot everything stays connected, for while walking one occupies the spaces between those interiors. One lives in the whole world rather than in interiors built up against it (Solnit 2021, 9).

Metal boxes in traffic. Metal boxes in parking lots. Metal boxes waiting in drive-throughs. Metal boxes stopping to fill up at gas stations. Metal boxes mostly occupied by only one person. Most car drivers come from indoor environments (office, school, or store) and are en route to another indoor environment (home, restaurant, or gym). Breathe all of this deeply in and slowly out. I'm not apart from this, but I ask you to feel this tension with me. How could this behavior not significantly impact our capacity to more genuinely connect to one another, to our deeper selves, and to the needs and wisdom of the planet?

While we all might generally understand the effort and need for shelter and protecting our physical body from harsh environments, I think it is healthy to question how far we have taken it. Do the temptations and behaviors around all this false armor leave the human condition in no way prepared for the raw, wondrous, and sometimes fierce ways of nature and for what is authentically arising within? We are made to face the elements of the natural world. We are made to engage with spontaneous experiences that keep us open and awake. We are made to fall, get up, and adapt as we move through our outward and inward terrain.

BETWEEN YOUR ACHES AND MINE

Having walked thousands of miles moving solo and alongside others on foot, I have found that the art of walking or rolling naturally allows raw truths, healing, and trust to calmly rise to the surface. There's space when you move this way. The air and possibility between words or thoughts is far more expansive than when sitting indoors and across from one another. The air and outdoor environment helps hold and process what begins to come to the surface. Imperfections dance with the swinging of your arms.

When there is conflict in my field of human relationships, I always try to leave the door open for the possibility of "walking it out." As I have learned to honor, live into, and defend what feels true for me, I tend to lose people I love. It breaks my heart every time. That said, when or if we can tremble and fumble together on a walk or roll together, days, weeks, or years later, it does wonders.

I believe humble movement reminds us that we are not stuck in pain, embarrassment, stress, grief, blame, or shame forever. It also reminds us to climb on down from any towers of right and wrong we might knowingly or unknowingly cling to.

> Now if I hear the sound of the genuine in me, and if you hear the sound of the genuine in you, it is possible for me to go down in me and come up in you. So that when I look at myself through your eyes having made that pilgrimage, I see in me what you see in me and the wall that separates and divides will disappear, and we will become one because the sound of the genuine makes the same music (Thurman 1980).

These words by Rev. Dr. Howard Thurman were written on the back of our wedding schedule, handed out to all our loved ones when Ben and I married each other in 2018. Our goddaughter, Alden, and two of our dearest friends, Meg and M.K., read it out loud to everyone as an invitation. I recite these words to myself and to the wind almost daily. My relationship to the sound of the genuine resembles a calmly spinning spiral. No arriving. Just dancing and swirling around it.

I invite you to reread Thurman's words again while imagining someone moving next to you, side by side. Imagine allowing more vulnerable truths to make their way to the surface, up through you and up through them. If they have any amount of love and care for you, they will more than likely continue moving with you, no matter how messy things get. If you have any amount of love and care for them, you will more than likely not physically abandon them. The embodiment of moving and being alongside allows what is genuine in yourself, what is genuine in whoever is with you, and what is genuine in all that moves between you, to more naturally appear.

I invite you now to release all the words. Vulnerability really needs to be lived and not explained. I send you compassionate encouragement to move with your own unique rumblings, as they are, as you are.

Into the field, together.

Into the spaces between your aches and mine.

Into the daunting and liberating frequency that weaves your dignity with mine.

Into a way of being that loves openly, courageously, tenderly, and unconditionally.

DEDICATED PRACTICE

Take some time to move with the practice below. Do you know the Indigenous tribal lands you are walking or rolling on? Learn from and honor them as you move. Listen to your body. Honor your needs. Honor the lived reality of all who walk or use a wheelchair as their primary form around you. Honor what will work for you, especially depending on your ability, community, and context. No rules. Only invitation.

—————— How Are We Really Doing? ——————

Vulnerability is fragile. Our wounds and deep truths are fragile. Other people's wounds and their deep truths are fragile. Go into this practice with grace, with space, and with great care.

Grounding Invitation: Start by taking a few deep breaths. If you imagine vulnerable things arising from the start, you might also place your hand on your heart or on the bark of a nearby tree alongside your breathing. From there, consider reading the following text to ground. If you are reading this as a collective of two or more people, replace *I* with *we* and *my* with *our*.

> As I invite vulnerability into my movement, I open, listen, tend to, and honor my fears, shame, anger, wounding, dreams, and all the things beyond all the words. I am moving with a recognition that what I might be suppressing, numbing, or running from might contribute to my own suffering and the suffering of others and the planet around me. I move with grace, humility, and self-compassion. I recognize this is a process, that I am "in process," and I am not expecting to arrive anywhere. Through courageous steps, unhurried movement, and a sky-filled, tree-filled, river-filled, people-filled field of possibility, I can begin to gently invite this often difficult, sometimes excruciating, and forever complex invitation of vulnerability.

Hand on Your Heart: Consider this invitation as complex, difficult, and tender things come up inside you, verbally from you, and audibly from another. Place your hand on your heart to remind yourself to breathe and to invite self-compassion. Allow this gesture to bring acceptance and care for all that is raw and real within you and those you move with.

I have included three different iterations for how you might move with our practice:

Solo: After the grounding invitation above, begin to slowly move. Allow any thoughts or tasks to slowly fall away. After you are ten to fifteen minutes in, ask yourself, "How am I doing?" Notice your response. Move with it. Hold it. Perhaps write a few words down. Walk or roll for a few more minutes. After some time has passed, take a deep breath. Listen more intently to your body and all your feelings, fears, and dreams living within you. As you continue, ask yourself, "How am I really doing?" Try to hold yourself to it. Notice what comes up. Notice what might feel scary, unsettling, uncomfortable, or liberating. Notice anger, sadness, desperation, numbness, exhaustion, fear, or shame. Allow tears. Allow frustration. Allow rage. Allow joy. Allow trembling. You might discern that you need to ask, or be asked by a witness, this question a third time, a fourth time, or any number of times to begin cracking through all the shells. Lean on a tree for comfort. Notice that you are still here and that your body is still moving. Listen for the need to stop and be with any one emotion that arises. This is not a pressure cooker. Hold all of this with compassion, space, and curiosity. You might try rereading the grounding invitation throughout your movement and as you close.

Solos in a Pair: Invite someone you trust to practice the solo invitation with you. Start together by reading the grounding practice to yourselves or out loud, perhaps each of you reading pieces. From there, move into your own solo practice. After an agreed upon amount of time, come back together and reflect, listen, and honor one another's experience.

Pair: Invite someone you trust to move with you. This will be a side-by-side, sharing, and listening frame. Consider reading the grounding invitation to yourselves or out loud beforehand. As you begin to move next to one another, start the process by asking, "How are you doing?" Listen, move, and respect whatever flows out of the person you are with. After a healthy amount of time, switch to have them ask you the same question. Be with and honor all that is shared. Do your best to be a present, conscious listener. When it feels right, pause your movement, and take a couple of deep breaths together. As you continue, ask, "How are you really doing?" Listen and nurture all that is shared. If you have time and are willing, you might benefit from moving through two or three more rounds where both of you ask one another this same question. Allow whatever fumbles out. Allow grunts and aches. Allow jumbled words. Allow tears and even screams. Allow silence. Be okay with never formally answering this question. Honor process and not arriving or solving. Honor where the question wants to take you. Close with love and compassion.

Time: Allow at least one to two hours. Any time of the day is okay, but cooler and more temperate conditions at sunrise or sunset can help to relax and nurture what the body, heart, and brain might need to support this invitation. If you are walking with someone, be extra sensitive to the timing and unique needs of who you will be walking with in terms of food, transportation, clothing, comfort, children, and other barriers or realities. Be flexible and open. Try to not have any hard lines around time before and after.

Location: Consider a quieter and more reflective location. A park is a perfect location as this is very much a walk that is honoring the inner journey, both in you and perhaps also in another. While the outer landscape will help hold what lives and aches on the inside, being extra mindful to care for and be present to whatever wants to surface is extra helpful. Try to avoid having your energy go to route safety or noisy distractions. All of that said, it sometimes needs to be right where you are, right from the front door. No rules.

Adaptation

Eye Contact: If you are moving with a loved one, try holding eye contact for a little longer when listening to them share. If you are feeling disconnection, you might benefit from prefacilitating: "Can we try something?" From there, if they are open, pause your movement, find a quiet place to sit, and face one another. From there, try to hold eye contact with no words for a full minute or longer. No rules. Blinking, turning away, and coming back is all a part of weaving trust and self-compassion. Notice what arises in you and in them.

7

WALKING AS PLAY

BECKONING THE INNER CHILD

As soon as they were dropped off, and after a few strange looks, we started moving. Within minutes they wanted to search for good walking sticks. I always had a walking stick with me, and they immediately wanted one too. Each of the boys, one seven and one nine, eventually found one that worked for them.

Their mom connected to our journey a couple of days prior and felt that it would be fun to have her boys join me for a few hours. I always love moving with young people in big open spaces. I had several parents, mostly homeschoolers, drop their kids off throughout my long walk. I remember always feeling awestruck and inspired by their level of trust. I learned quickly into my cross-country walk that nearly everyone, no matter the age, would eventually feel lighter and more themselves after a good fifteen to twenty minutes of movement.

As we moved, we talked about family, hobbies, and what excited each of them. The questions came rolling in.

What does Kanoa mean?

What does Kanoa eat?

Does he like kids?

Is he a wolf?

Do you ever ride on his back?

Can I ride on his back?

Where does he sleep?

Where do you sleep?

How big are your feet?

Where do you pee?

What do you eat?

Why do you walk so much?

There was no shame in any question.

Do you ever accidently poop on your shoes?

In less than an hour, we were singing, laughing, and stopping to explore everything that showed up along the road. We were alive. They climbed on hills. I would follow. Their eyes would widen at the sight of slowly moving beetles. So would mine. They examined an old rusty toy that was tossed out of a car window. I was curious with them. They yelled and sang so I yelled and sang. They pretended their sticks were swords, so I did the same. Play and wonder spilled from their pores. It also started to spill from mine. What could I climb next? What could we explore together?

We saw a snake slither away and watched it until we couldn't see it anymore. We stopped to look at flowers and bugs. We threw rocks at nearby fence posts. The first one to hit the post three times won. We had colorful and lengthy conversations with the cows and horses we passed along the way. We dug up dirt and took breaks under trees.

I learned so much from these two.

In just two hours, we found a way to connect and play beyond the world of cars, walls, screens, and rigid relationships to time. I was reminded of how dull adulting has become. Even as I work to break free from so many molds on this walk, the two boys made it clear just how much I was still missing. There were and are so many opportunities around us to be in constant wonder and play.

At the two-hour mark, the youngest one was done. His face started to cave in, and the moping began. It was time for mom to pick them up. As she drove away, they held onto their sticks in the back seat while waving out the windows, screaming, "Good-bye, Kanoa!" Kanoa really was the star.

JUMP, KICK, CLIMB, SWIRL, AND SING

Have you ever slowed down enough to really see the way the sun glows on and around flowing grass during a sunset? It always captivates me. There was no shortage of this walking through the rural Midwest on my cross-country walk. In addition to the grasses, I found great joy in the way large rolled up hay bales would shine like buckets of gold, almost like they lived at the end of their own rainbows. I often wanted to hop the fence and run to them. While walking in eastern Kansas, my friend Lacey and I did just that.

We climbed up on top of them and stretched our arms wide open, inviting endless horizons of farmland into our gaze. We sang. We laughed. We shouted. We balanced and rolled on the bales with our feet. We posed for photos with blazing purple, red, pink, and orange skies behind us. No one was around. We were wild and free in our own imaginative and playful world.

We must find ways to sideline the heavy, overthinking, and overconforming part of our brains. Arms up and out. Dancing hips and legs. Music, costumes, and jumping. Life is not easy for most of us, and moving our bodies as a pathway to, can I say, *shake shit off*, is necessary, life-giving, and liberating. Parades, demonstrations, protests, and outdoor gatherings and celebrations that involve movement of any kind help us tap into just how much human movement frees up one's body, one's pain, one's joy, and one's sense of agency.

Movement that involves play and body expression gives us permission not to be limited or confined to how one "should" express themselves, engage the world around them, and exist in this one precious life. While play can be seen or assumed as lighthearted, adventurous, and joyful, it is also revolutionary inside a culture that has placed an oppressive amount of worthiness and value on conforming to various forms of order and tidiness.

Keep looking to children.

Notice and absorb how they genuinely navigate an environment. They jump, crawl, explore, pick up, carry, throw, dance, sing, dig, kick, and climb without much hesitation. Walking and rolling in one's environment, with the intention to break out of norms, is such an important invitation to feel more human and alive in this time. Next time you are out, pick up that stick, sing that song, jump on that bench, and swing those arms. Organize your people. Speak your truth with your movement, body, and breath. Move, twirl, and heal. Hold your hopes high and make patterns with it in the sand. Tap the fence and hug trees. Kids will notice right away and will love you for it.

INTEGRATION PRACTICE:
GET WET

On your walk, seek to engage and connect with water in playful ways. Take your shoes off and splash in nearby puddles or on the edges of streams and rivers. Kneel and be extra curious about all the details under, near, and around the water. Notice the glimmer of light and all the wavy reflections. Feel the water. If it's fresh running water, dunk your head in or splash the water up to your face. If you are with someone, you might as well splash them, too. Bring an inflatable tube with you. Get wet, and let the wisdom and gifts of water nourish you.

MOVEMENT AS LOVE, PLAY, AND LIBERATION

The following story is from one of my most cherished friends and teachers, Rev. Dr. Dawn Riley Duval. She has taught me more than I could ever put into words. Her work with Soul 2 Soul Sisters and her vibration in the world is emergent, loving, and courageous.

I love to swim and go on long hikes with loved ones. My knowing of love and liberation through movement was ignited when I was a little girl. Some of my fondest memories include watching my parents teach aerobics classes to a gym full of beautiful Black people—all body shapes, the full spectrum of melanin, various ages—at the beloved Skyland Recreation Center, located in the heart of the Park Hill neighborhood in Denver, which was then a predominantly Black neighborhood. On Monday, Wednesday, and Friday evenings the exercise classes were an entire Black experience full of bright lights, blaring funky music, loud sentiments of instruction and encouragement from my parents, loud complaints or celebrations in response, sweat flying, blood flowing, energy bouncing off the walls, hearts pounding, laughter, fussin' ... all while the children, including myself, sat on blue gym mats and ate snacks, completed homework, played, and watched our beloveds work out.

Before and after classes, Mom and Dad connected with each member of the village, asking about and offering guidance regarding physical, emotional, and spiritual health and eating habits. My parents' relational and joyful care for community members' health and wellness made me proud. To me, it felt like church. Full-body praying. Holistic. Healthy. Helpful. Holy. From my parents' modeling, I learned and discerned that I too would care for, journey with, and lovingly lead my people in ways that felt like blissful Black villages.

I was nine years old when I decided to join the Colorado Flyers Track Team. My teammates and I worked out for three to four hours each day, six days per week. It took a few years for my brain and gangly limbs to finally coordinate and translate all that hard work to wins at track meets. Because of my height and speed, the event that chose me was the hundred-meter hurdles. I competed in this awesome event through middle school, high school, college, and as a professional, I even competed in the USA Olympic Trials in 1996 and 2000. I loved the hurdles. Imagine the total body synchronicity that is required to sprint over ten hurdles: awesome attention to technique, the courage and creativity to fly while sprinting, audacious in taking risks to win races and receive prizes. And I adored how my body felt. Every muscle strong and ready. Healthy. So damn powerful. Hydrated. Energized. I impressed myself and I loved that. Rested. Joyful. Fearless. *Free.* The privilege of experiencing this high level of good health for much of my life causes me to be passionate about leading work that helps Black women experience sustained health, movement, wellness, and joy.

In addition to the glory of movement, I have learned and deeply experienced the vulnerability and helplessness of being seriously ill. Eighteen years ago—when I was in seminary and won an internship with the Red Cross in Namibia, Africa—pulmonary emboli developed in my lungs, and I had to be emergency transported to the States. Two years later, while in the hospital recovering after the birth of my son, I began having horrendous pain in my head. Scans revealed that blood clots were forming in my brain. Due to the reoccurrence of blood clots, I will take blood thinners each day for the rest of my life. During my second pregnancy, I gave myself daily heparin injections to counter blood clots. Additionally, following the killings of Aiyana Stanley-Jones, Trayvon Martin, Rekia Boyd, Michael Brown, Sandra Bland, and so many other Black beloveds, I have battled depression, insomnia, exhaustion, and gastric ulcers. During my healing and health journey, I have experienced so many medical professionals who ignored or downplayed my pain. So, I fight for birth justice, reproductive justice, and Black Liberation. I want Black women to soulfully heal, play, move, and receive loving health care from Black women who adore us and want us to thrive.

INVITING EASE

Rev. Dr. Dawn offers us such an important story on love, play, health, and justice. In the wake of these soulful words, she also highlights the devastation to her own body and the greater community related to systemic oppression, chronic pain, and illness. Play is complex and unique to each of our bodies, environments, and circumstances. I believe there is a great confluence where play rushes into the nourishing waters of rest. It feels a little like putting your feet into the creek after a good long walk. It is playful, restoring, and healing all in one.

Moving in an unhurried way helps us let go of pressure. It also, even if just for a moment, gives us tools to detach our worthiness from production and consumption. It invites us, more naturally, to open our eyes, swing our arms, listen to our hearts, and feel our senses. Rest and play can slowly unfold if we give ourselves time for it. How can you add fifteen minutes or one hour to your commute or your day to honor these important human gifts? Next time you go out, bring things that can make play or rest easy: blankets, hula hoops, bubbles, jump ropes, roller blades, frisbees, hammocks, coloring books, and sweatshirts for extra comfort and to roll up as pillows.

As someone who has walked and rolled with thousands of people from all over the world, varying in age, background, pace, and ability, I am always overwhelmed with what play and rest can stir up in the human heart, in our relationships, and with our connection to the planet. Whether it is flying a kite or quietly napping under a tree next to a friend, movement in the outside world can inspire a million portals to trust and connection. Be open to how play can bring moments of lightness and joy. Honor how rest and ease can nourish your weariness.

DEDICATED PRACTICE

Take some time to move with the practice below. Do you know the Indigenous tribal lands you are walking or rolling on? Learn from and honor them as you move. Listen to your body. Honor your needs. Honor the lived reality of all who walk or use a wheelchair as their primary form around you. Honor what will work for you, especially depending on your ability, community, and context. No rules. Only invitation.

Gifts, Naps, and Surprises

Seeking play and rest alongside unhurried movement can do wonders for your blazing beautiful heart and for all you might connect with along the way.

Grounding: Take a few deep breaths before you journey out. If you can, try to be outside and look up at the sky. Notice any clouds or tall trees. Invite curiosity and openness into your movement. Invite compassion for your story, body, and life experiences.

Movement: Take some time to just read through the examples I have offered below. Feel them and invite them into your own context. They do not need to be social and loud. They do not need to be anything but honoring to your body, your environment, and your lived experience. My main invitation is for you to be open to the spontaneous, to surprise, and to what might invite you to play or rest in any given moment as you move.

- **Invite families with children:** If you are open and available to play, curiosity, and wonder, you will have more than enough to work with.

- **Sidewalk chalk:** Bring chalk with you and write, draw, and craft meaningful messages, affirmations, and symbols that inspire, encourage, or even challenge people. Try interactive chalk designs like hopscotch or labyrinths.

- **Earth naps:** As you move, seek out a spot to restfully lay your body on the Earth. I highly recommend under a large mature tree. Bring a blanket. Bring a small pillow or scrunch up a sweatshirt for head support. Notice the branches. Notice the clouds. Protect time to lie, open, and be.

- **Gifting and art:** One of my passionate walking friends, Nicole Huguenin, is always coming up with creative "gifts and surprises" while moving in public spaces. In honor of her, you might bring with you small gifts to pass out to people while you walk: affirmation notes, small art pieces, offerings or blessings, handmade jewelry. You might also stuff your bag with art supplies and find various areas to plop down and make art, inviting others who pass by to join you.

- **Music and dance:** Play or connect a speaker alongside your movement to invite the gifts of music. Invite others. Do it solo. Create a playlist with your favorite dance music or music that is calming and grounding. Dress up! Try it as a "glow-in-the-dark dance walk," which can be great for kids, families, and neighborhoods.

- **Boulders, trees, hills, and walls:** As you move, look for ways you can engage your environment in playful or restful ways. Climb or lean on nearby boulders. Swing from or lean on trees. Make your way up or roll down hills if you are able. Balance on walls, rails, curbs, ramps, and stairs. Invite curiosity and exploration alongside all that is around you.

- **Hammocks and fold-up chairs:** Bring a light tie-up hammock or a light fold-up chair that can fit in a pack or be easily carried. Start with ten to fifteen minutes of movement to open your senses beforehand. From there, seek places that inspire ease and rest.

Location: If you are doing this with hopes of public engagement, try to have your walk, roll, or activity in a popular park, plaza, or walkway. If you are doing it solo, truly anywhere works. Mix up your locations and practices to see what shows up in different scenarios.

Time: Aim for at least twenty to thirty minutes of movement before or during the practice so you can create new pathways and find good flow.

my universe
& my truths
are not made
to fit inside the
boxes
that
keep
you
from
yours

8

WALKING AS RESISTANCE

MOVING WITH PRIDE

The parade is starting. I can already see the rainbow balloons high in the air between the mature trees on Denver's Franklin Street. They are making their way from Cheesman Park in the heart of the Mile High City.

I see glimpses of floats, waving arms, and big hair. We are surrounded by every kind of love relationship under the sun. All shapes, sizes, colors, races, genders and no genders, sexual orientations, languages, cultures, ages, abilities, and more make their way out to see and be seen. Hot pink hair spikes. Large bright red lips. Boots and motorbikes. Leather, vests, and ties. Shirts, no shirts. High heels for days. Swirling bodies dancing and prancing. Tight ripped jean shorts. Black Lives Matter posters. Water and pipeline justice banners. Indigenous #LandBack campaigns. Earth care petitions. Christian-identifying parents hugging LGBTQIA2S+ kids who were cut off from their families. Bubbles and tails.

I love when I see tails. I hope to wear a tail someday.

Many speak with color and flare. Many are not there. Many may never connect to a more public path of expression. It does not matter.

As I watch everyone flow and move around me to the sound of their own drum, I pull my shorts up a little higher and release an extra button on the shirt. I love wearing drawstring shorts well above the knee, with wavy mostly unbuttoned shirts. I love the way the wind feels wrapping itself around my upper thighs and chest. It makes me feel more a part of everything around me. I do long to express myself more with what I wear and how I present. More earrings. More necklaces. More bracelets. More tattoos. More dancing. More eyeliner. Soon? Maybe. Someday? Maybe.

Pride expression is so radically unique to each precious being. We are an ocean of revealing, emerging, and existing. That is what I love. A courageous and tender "be you" ripples and swirls in the air. Pride, for me, is well beyond the parade and the month of June. It is an ongoing unfolding of being in love with and awake to how I feel, how I want to express myself, and how I ache to move through relationships and the world.

I am fully out to friends, family, and the greater public. I have been for many years. Some fully celebrate with me. Some express love but never ask. Some don't know what to feel or believe, so they avoid the topic or avoid me altogether. Some quietly shame and judge. Some put up walls and turn away. Some condemn, dehumanize, and hate.

As you picked up already from the introduction, my coming-out journey was far from easy. It nearly ended me. I know this impacts my complex journey to express myself more freely. Perhaps it always will.

I really enjoy holding my husband's hand. It feels so easy and right on the inside. I naturally want to put my legs on his while sitting on a plaza bench. I want to place my arm around his shoulders when waiting in line or enjoying a meal at a restaurant. I want to kiss him, and I want him to kiss me while in line at the store or riding the bus. I want us to stare into each other's eyes freely, no matter who is around us. On rare occasions I push through, allowing this to come forth, but usually only for a moment. I am quick to retreat and cover up what wants to be expressed for the sake of others, toxic norms, and the twisted exhaustion of it all. For me, honestly, it is hard to know what is more exhausting: to suppress or to push through.

As hundreds of people walk and roll by us, I am reminded of how walking repeatedly saves me. It anchors me in radical belonging. It reminds me to continue resisting oppressive forces, limitations, and expectations of others.

Moving through the world with just my body and a backpack moves me into a world of wonder and color. As I breathe and participate with my surroundings, I move and process complex dreams and stress while leaning on the gifts of nature's nonbinary, colorful, and expressive existence. It isn't about solving or fixing or arriving. It all just moves with me and is more easily cared for or released. It has room to grow new branches and to seek more nourishment. Instead of sitting in a large hole somewhere in my heart, mind, or neck, it flows out into my arms and my art. When someone is moving with me, I feel each of our complex inner stories turning into a valley of rivers and streams. Slowly, stone by stone, tree by tree, brook by brook, we can reveal and trust new and creative forms of love and belonging.

Here they come. All in rows. Twenty or so people from every background under the sun move with grace and ease in front of me. They must have rehearsed for months. They are all holding wands with colorful ribbons. "Like a Prayer" Madonna magic echoes all around them. Knees and feet lifting and twisting. Arms and togetherness, blazing trails of color and confidence for all to see. Thousands of children, parents, friends, and stories move and dance and sing.

As I watch, I keep reflecting on the power of large bodies of people walking and rolling together—in prideful celebration, in protest and direct action, in silence and grief, in pilgrimage and prayer, in escape and refuge. When waves of people gather to move alongside one another, the world watches. They are a force. Time bends and tunes to their aches and drums. Walking as resistance is an epic and profound invitation.

I'm sitting in the grass watching it all go by. For me, it is far easier and more natural to observe and draw from other people who shine and sparkle on center stage. I can absorb their magic and find my own ways to let it spill out.

While I honor and love this, I do actually dream of getting up off the damn grass. I fantasize about jolting up, unbuttoning whatever shirt I'm wearing, embracing my not-six-pack stomach, rolling up my shorts, and walking with this chorus of beautiful light. Whether I do it or not, I recognize it is important for me to dream and to see myself up there and out there.

I am the ocean.

I am the rainbow.

I am the diva.

I am my pain.

I am my joy.

I am my weaknesses.

I am my attractions.

I am my curves.

I am my grief.

I am my gifts.

I am radical love.

I am queer, gay, LGBTQIA2S+.

I am woven with all who have been harmed by heteronormative oppression.

I am woven with all who have been shamed by toxic patriarchal systems and behaviors.

I am woven with all who have felt unworthy, unseen, and disregarded by exclusive religion.

I am woven with all who have nearly died under the choke hold of white supremacy.

I am woven with all who have been wounded by wounded people.

I am woven into a wondrous "love is love" misfit tapestry.
I am a miracle of moments.
I am.

HONOR THY ACHE

As someone who fights being put into any one box, being typed
an Enneagram nine with an eight wing nailed my lifelong coping
mechanisms to the wall. As I have learned more about this spacious,
beautiful, and troubling "peacemaker" identity, it is no surprise that
I have had a steady and deeply rooted relationship to suppressing
what is really going on inside me. I mastered the art of "stuffing
things down" all throughout my childhood.

Keep the peace, Jonathon. Avoid conflict at all costs, Jonathon.
Do not, Jonathon, be the reason there is conflict in the world. Be the
one that everyone loves and depends on all the time. Be good, nice,

and stable. Absorb communal, relational, and planetary grief for all your days, turn it into good, and abandon your own truths, pain, anger, and joy. Harmony, always.

Fuck that.

Oh, that felt good. Here it usually comes—the great domino effect. What will people think?

Fuck that too.

"Yes," my trembling stomach cheers. "Again!"

Fuck that!

Ah, it gives me life to say it. To feel it. To own in.

My life as a peacemaker is also true, purposeful, and incredibly genuine. I do seek peace for all people. I long for harmony in all things. Witnessing and affirming grief in the world and in others is profoundly precious to me. Helping others feel deeply and fully seen is one of the greatest gifts of my life.

All of that said, I don't need to absorb and bury it all. Conflict is healthy and necessary. Movement into and with tension is healthy and necessary. I also promised myself in those final weeks of my cross-country walk that I would continue "taking myself on long walks" to stay close to and to honor my own imperfect truths, pains, boundaries, and dreams. I never want to feel far from what aches on the inside.

I sometimes visualize these long walks as digging down into deeper soil. With each step or roll, the shovel breaks up crusty concrete bullshit that keeps me from being more honest, alive, and awake. It rumbles the ground. It invites necessary tension. It has the chance to bring us together around what is raw, painful, wondrous, and possible.

Hello resistance.

You terrify me, and I need you.

You nurture my wounds and give breath to my truths.

You are blazing love for all.

Moving my body in an unhurried way is its own form of resistance. As my human frame humbly moves, I have time to process, listen, and tend to my stress, fears, aches, and dreams. This kind of resistance—resistance to staying busy, always going fast, working the machine, and suppressing what is real—defies all that wants to separate me from you and the planet.

MY VERY BODY

As we invite the notion of our very bodies moving in the outside world as a form of resistance, I want us to weave in personal, social, and political themes and have shared a few ways this shows up for me.

Personal

Personal resistance can move through us in a variety of ways. In addition to what I shared related to pride, it often shows up for me in the context of moving my body on foot against the forces of heavy traffic on large, busy, and practical arterial streets. Human bodies are out here trying to catch the bus. Human bodies are out here trying to get home, to work, and to school. As I move, I feel myself literally cutting the thick, artificial air of fast-moving automobiles.

> As cars fly by ...
> My body still moves and breathes.
> I am the Earth, storm, sun, deer, and star.
> See my fragile and powerful human frame.
> Witness my existence.

Traffic blazes from the front. Traffic blazes from behind. It's everywhere. If we allow the resistance to be felt, we can find our place in the great circle. This great circle shows us that we are all harmed by streets and systems that disregard the natural world and those who walk or roll for health, connection, and transportation. My very body is a form of personal resistance.

Social

I care so much about people moving with other people. Whether it is romantic connection, conflict care, or playful expression, there is so much around us diminishing our capacity to be with one another "in real life." I find that organizing, inviting, and shaping walking or rolling experiences with groups, with the family, with colleagues, or with one another is, in and of itself, a form of social protest. It moves against the grind of devastating isolation and disconnection. Moving in this way weaves us together rather than giving ourselves completely away to flimsy, temporary, divisive, and transactional time. My very body is a form of social resistance.

Political

With so much unfaced, unhealed, and unrepaired pain in the world, we must have ways to collectively rise and move the hurt. I have always felt a couple of feet off the ground when walking in and with protest. Unchecked power is an ugly, oppressive, self-serving shadow that will stay high up in the tower as long as it is able. If there are not movements of people with their courageous bodies literally rumbling the ground, how could justice ever be seen, felt, or possible?

Whether you organize a small protest for your local community or participate in a large march in a nearby city, moving with an ocean of people demanding justice is a force. Everyone near it stops. Whether people agree or not, waves of collective resistance break the mundane and shake the ground one stands on. Human bodies have walked, rolled, and sweated their way into more just treatment, changes in policy, and granting of dignity and rights in a variety of ways because of political protest. My very body is a form of political resistance.

INTEGRATION PRACTICE:
RESISTANCE TO SPEED

This practice is primarily for people who drive as their primary form and those who influence decisions impacting city, county, state, and federal transportation systems.

Protect some time to walk or roll next to a busy, practical arterial street. These are generally large high-speed commercial corridors or small highways dotted with grocery stores, strip malls, hospitals, banks, libraries, schools, and bus stops. Try to make it a route that you are familiar with or take often in your vehicle. If you are moving along a roadway that does not have sidewalks, it is the safest to move against traffic so you can more easily see and be seen. Prioritize your safety. Wear bright clothing, comfortable shoes, and if you can, invite someone to move with you to increase visibility and support. As you move, specifically open your senses to what it feels like to have so many fast-moving cars rush past you. Notice your unhurried human frame withstanding forces that blaze past you. Feel your courage as you continue moving against a system that wants you to speed up, bypass, and dismiss anything that gets in your way. Notice the sounds. Notice the smells. Notice what becomes available to you as you slow down and move with a landscape you have always driven through. What are you learning, in your body and awareness, related to accessibility, nature, and public health? As you continue to move, imagine elders, children, people with disabilities, and those who have no choice but to be moving on these corridors in all conditions. Close with deep breaths, reflection on what you experienced, and any notes on how you might take action toward healing and repair.

How might you embody resistance with your very body? What does it look like for you to reclaim or connect to a more unhurried pace in your unique life and environment? Move with how you and those around you can be agents of personal, social, and political movement and disruption.

THE GRIEF OF BYPASSING

As someone who moves through the world primarily by foot or by bus, my insides constantly twist up at all that gets destroyed and avoided in the wake of "faster" and "more is better." It is faster for me to message you through a screen than walk over or handwrite you a letter. It is faster for me to get more and do more if I drive instead of walk, bike, roll, or take the bus. I must work more, drive faster, and park closer so I can quickly pay for more things. It is faster for me to microwave my food, have my food delivered by car, and buy more in bulk instead of growing, preparing, and making it myself.

These are sweeping generalizations, and there are grave inequities deep inside of scarcity-influenced capitalism, unchecked classism, and ongoing systemic racism that make living outside of these ideas terribly difficult and even unsafe for so many. I also don't pretend for one second not to be a part of it. I get lost in faster is better, more is better all the time.

I am, however, committed to unapologetically name and invite the grief I feel, as I walk for hours and hours on our beloved Earth, related to so much outrageous and irresponsible behavior.

I think it is also important to invite the notion that bypassing isn't always related to speed. Picture millions of cars idling on pavement all over the world. On any given day I will walk by hundreds of individuals sitting in their cars waiting for stop lights, waiting in drive-throughs, waiting in rush hour traffic, and waiting in parking lots. Time, nature, community, and a more wholesome sense of belonging blur into the background behind so many demoralizing layers of disconnection.

I invite you to pause and invite the words "the grief of bypass-ing" into your space again. Say it to yourself and perhaps again out loud. Try to feel what these words want to draw out of you and out of us. Cry if you need to. Scream and howl if you need to. Where might you connect to a sense of sorrow or frustration around all that gets missed, lost, or even destroyed when we physically fly past or block a blossoming and breathing world?

Slowing down, growing our own food, healing our bodies, sim-plifying our consumption, repairing systemic injustice, and protect-ing time to rest is a direct threat. To not bypass is a threat. There is so much, in us and outside us, calling for our care and attention.

If we are to move into this deep and complex grief with care and compassion, we must find creative ways to heal and resist. If we are ever to turn away from the many temptations, strings, and efforts to have us bypass what is deep within us and all around us, we must find creative ways to heal and resist. Moving, humbly moving, with this grief is available to each of us. We are not the strings that others pull. We are dynamic, fluid, loving, wounded, imperfect, and radi-ant agents of emergence. We can, humbly and boldly, walk or roll ourselves into being the change we want to see.

DEDICATED PRACTICE

Take some time to move with the practice below. Do you know the Indigenous tribal lands you are walking or rolling on? Learn from and honor them as you move. Listen to your body. Honor your needs. Honor the lived reality of all who walk or use a wheelchair as their primary form around you. Honor what will work for you, especially depending on your ability, community, and context. No rules. Only invitation.

───────────────── Making Waves ─────────────────

The invitations below are meant to help inspire your own versions of personal, social, and political protest. We desperately need creative invitation and movement that moves our own cosmic color, truths, and authentic forms of expression into the world. We also need creative invitation and movement to trouble the waters under who or what is hurting our hearts and violating indisputable codes related to human and planetary atrocity.

Grounding: Before setting out on any one of the invitations below, I invite you and perhaps whoever you are with to find an area close to nature. This could be a flowing stream, a mature tree, wildflowers, or just the dirt under your feet. You might kneel to place your hand on the roots of a tree, on the soil itself, or in the flowing water. Close your eyes and take several deep breaths. Ask the core of the Earth and all created life around you to nourish your movement, to give you courage, and to ripple out from your movement. Ask nature to help shake up oppressive systems and inspire compassion and justice. Honor your body, your breathing, and all your unique life experiences.

The following three areas include only ideas and seeds. Mix them. Change them. Adapt them. Consider inviting someone you trust to join and witness you.

Personal Resistance: This invitation is rooted in resisting all that attempts to box up or shut down your color, art, aches for justice, pain, dreams, grief, joy, song, and so on. It can be in what you wear (clothing, makeup, hair, shoes, style, hats, wigs, wings, tails), how you identify or present (gender, nonbinary, identity, drag), what you want to speak or perform (poems, quotes, songs, skits, protest, justice), how you move or honor your body (dance, rest, walking or rolling against speed or traffic), or any other frame or theme that feels expressive, authentic, and life-giving. This does not need to be loud or performative. It can be more subtle and radically meaningful to you.

Social Resistance: This is primarily rooted in resisting defaults to sit indoors or meet behind screens as default or primary forms of connecting with one another. The following ideas can be applied to neighbors, family, friends, colleagues, company meetings, community groups, and more.

- **Movement Meetings:** Scout one or two routes around where your group, family, company, or friends traditionally meet, or a neutral space if it's local but usually virtual. Have a couple of thirty-minute or one-hour options, perhaps at local parks, in neighborhoods, or on a greenway trail. Have a couple of prompting connection questions in mind as you ground and begin to walk or roll. Consider the pace and comfort of the group. Do you know where there are places to break, rest, or use the restroom?

- **Neighborhood Walks or Rolls:** Create a weekly or monthly walking or rolling group specifically for the purposes of engaging your neighbors. You might commit to three or six months so you can discern how it is working for you. Pick a day, time, and location that is easy for you since you will be committing to leading or hosting it, at least initially. Be as specific as you can in your intention around pace, time, meeting location, and purpose. Come up with a catchy name. When people gather, do an introduction circle. As you move, you might have folks switch who they are connecting with halfway through or several times throughout your walk. Engage people you pass by or encounter. You might hand them small flyers inviting them to your next walk. When you finish, offer some time for announcements and further connection. Eventually have others cohost alongside you.

Political Resistance: Seek collective movement alongside campaigns and issues you care about. There are so many ways to get involved and support political resistance. I have offered two ideas for specifically weaving the gifts of political resistance through human movement:

- **Engage in Public Movement:** Join, help organize, and invite others to move with you alongside already scheduled protests, direct actions, marches, and gatherings. Protect time to specifically make yourself available to walk or roll with what is being organized. Notice and absorb what it feels like to be among waves of human bodies moving together in collective activism. Document by video, audio, photography, sketch, or poetry some of your experience to share with, invite, and inspire people in your network and local news outlets.

- **Invite Your People:** Organize your friends, neighbors, school groups, or local networks to walk or roll while (a) publicly supporting larger protests or direct actions with signs, chants, and demands at specific locations such as popular streets, around or to city halls, through large public parks, or (b) more intimately engaging in side-by-side moving dialogue with prompts, questions, and guidance around specific resistance-related topics.

Safety and Experimentation: As you try on one or several of the invitations listed in this larger practice, I highly recommend inviting people to join you. There are many voices, both external and internal, that want to crush resistance expression. Root into experimentation. It doesn't have to be over-planned or over-the-top in any way. It also doesn't have to be done the way others do it. Be creative, emergent, and open. Some experiments will be life-giving, and some won't fit. Honor it all as it shows up.

   Location and Timing: Try this anywhere and everywhere for as long as you want. If you want this to be publicly witnessed or engaged, make your route along a commonly used corridor (main streets, popular public plazas, or popular vehicle traffic) or a public park.

find your people & find your magic

9

WALKING AS CREATIVE WONDER

BOTTLE WALLS AND ROOF STARS

We started to approach her property. I loved it right away. It was creative, full of dirt, and natural. There was nothing inauthentic about it. It ached with aged artistic expression and the footprints of people and plants constantly in process. Nothing was static or controlled.

As we turned the corner, my cousin Matt, who joined me for three weeks, and I stood there for a moment and stared into the large blue glass-bottle sculpture wall that must have stood ten or fifteen feet high. Just next to the bottle wall was a beautiful chandelier hanging from a wise old tree that reached over her outdoor dining table. Underneath the table were several large worn rugs. They were spread out under the table with an assortment of random chairs circled around it. Some were wood. Some were metal. I will never forget all the colors.

We sat at the table and connected. The sun would shine through the glass. It sprayed color and creative permission all over our sweaty and exhausted skin. I looked up at the old tree as I felt the cool dirt under my drying feet. I was overwhelmed with how much I loved her place and how she and others expressed creative freedom.

Reaching Moab, Utah, and staying with Teri on day 167 of my cross-country walk was a dream come true. So many of my drawings as a kid reflected dreams of flying out of suburbia and living in open, creative, communal, and mystical worlds. As I continued to mosey around her creative space, I felt like I could take deeper and more honest breaths.

Before the sun went down, we walked over to visit her art studio in a cozy barnlike structure. She had quite the collection of brushes, paints, canvases, natural objects, stones, and glues spread out everywhere. There was also an outfitted bus in the back of the property where people in transition could stay for various stretches of time. It was unquestionable to her to have a place that would be shared with people like me passing through and people in need.

Her big project was finishing the build-out of her creative open-air home. She had been working on it for years. The draft coming through her not-yet-covered walls and unfinished beams was amazing. We sat on the weathered couch near the half-working kitchen as she showed us what she was currently working on.

Teri carried herself so freely and openly. She knew who she was. She radiated with permission to be okay in and even enjoy always being "in process." That night, my cousin and I rolled out our sleeping bags on her roof and slept under the stars.

We rose with the sun and headed out early. As we slowly walked away, I looked back and took a deep breath in, hoping I would never forget her or this incredible blanket of moments. I left Teri's place feeling full of creative permission. I promised myself that I would forever listen to what stirs and dreams and tugs in my creative heart. I also promised myself to commit to always seek a third way, a way in between the lines, a way that honors awe, hospitality, compassion, creative expression, wildness, wonder, human dignity, and possibility. Thank you, Teri.

STUMBLING UPON

If it wasn't for approaching each day by foot, I would never have found my way into Teri's story and magic-filled existence. Our pace and unhurried relationship to time allowed us to be more fully available to spontaneous encounters. You don't have to walk or roll across state lines. It doesn't have to be overseas. There is magic and wonder all around us. There are numerous stories, exchanges, and unexpected surprises right out your door, right where you live, that exist to be shared and seen.

The night before staying in Teri's high desert dreamscape, we connected with a family who stopped on the side of the road to check on us. They passed us on their way into town and decided to purchase a two-gallon jug of grape juice for our journey. While we were both deeply grateful, we kindly declined to carry it. We did ask if we could fill up our water bottles with it. As we took a break and chugged grape juice, we all sat on the side of the road and continued to connect. Within fifteen minutes they invited us to stay at their home and have dinner together. Three hours later we arrived at their home in Castle Valley. When they opened the door, you could hear what sounded like a jungle from inside the house. This amazing family had at least thirty or forty exotic birds. Cages everywhere. The sounds. The flight. The poop. The best part was watching two small parrots twist their legs in my cousin's hair. Once they had good footing with enough hair wrapped around their tiny legs, they would throw themselves out into the air. They were cleaning, or perhaps preening, their feathers while still tethered to his locks. The birds remained in his hair as we sat and shared a meal together. As he was buttering his bread, they would continue to dive in all directions. We slept like rocks, and the next morning they took us on a three-hour float trip on the Colorado River.

Every day on my cross-country walk, and on any walk since, there are gifts, surprises, and encounters that would have been impossible to predict. This is one of the main reasons I have made walking a necessary tool to inspire creativity, imagination, and inspiration. This is not solely a product of my artist identity or being on a special mission. It is about trusting movement, changing my relationship to time, and removing what keeps me from being more open. Who or what will I stumble upon today that will surprise me, inspire me, and nourish me in ways I could never predict?

INTEGRATION PRACTICE:
A MOVING CANVAS

As you plan for your walk or roll, bring a few art supplies with you: a sketch book, paints, sidewalk chalk, pencils, a camera, a journal, a musical instrument. Allow your movement to inspire and invite creativity. You might place your sketchbook in your hand to make it extra easy to stop and sketch something that captures your attention. Plan to take several breaks to make art. Try not to overthink or overprepare. Be okay with just a couple of artistic tools. The main goal is to free up and inspire your heart, body, and creative process through movement. Your art can represent moments, physical objects, or landscapes around you. Your art can also be from your imagination, as walking or rolling can help clear out things that block us from tapping into our imagination. Be open to experimenting with multiple forms of art-making in one go. At the end, you might have a couple of sketches, a poem, and new dance moves. Also, be patient with the creative process, as there can be so much blocking our capacity to feel and express creativity. Keep moving and keep opening. Your art for the day may rest in a meaningful journal entry observing what you saw and how it felt to move. Close with gratitude and a couple of deep breaths.

NOURISHING OUR SPARK

Walking is a ten- to twenty-minute neurological gateway to creativity. This is not just a nice idea. It is not a fad. If we are to be of a way that can more readily emerge from tired patterns, and imagine a more nurturing world, we need to activate the very system we've been working with for thousands of years. Our capacity to be creative, open, and expansive needs our time and an incredible amount of movement. Shane O'Mara, neurologist and author of *In Praise of Walking,* shares,

> Walking places greater demands on the body and brain. More oxygen is needed, and greater activity is required across many different brain systems to ensure that you don't fall over, so that you can see where you are going, and to coordinate your limbs. Then you must make quick micro decisions about the direction

of travel—even if it is just a circumnavigation of your office. A simple, collateral effect of rising and moving is that activity spreads across more distant brain regions—increasing the likelihood that half-thoughts and quarter-ideas, sitting below consciousness, can come together in new combinations. The regularity of the rhythm of walking itself, paced by the spinal cord's pattern generators, coupled with a deemphasis on time, and time itself, perhaps provides a good way to kick-start the kind of creative thinking we all need (O'Mara 2019, 155).

We need more movement to help care for our bodies. We need more movement to help tend to our relationships. We desperately need creative movement to help us bravely imagine where we go from here as participants in public, social, corporate, and planetary systems. O'Mara continues, "There's a powerful lesson to be learned here: those charged with complex political, organizational, and other problems should not be cooped up in conference rooms. They should get out and walk their way to better solutions, and to a better world" (O'Mara 2019, 155). Where can you protect more time and take more risks to move your people? How can you inspire and ignite creative possibility with your family, peers, colleagues, public leaders, local schools, and greater community?

INTEGRATION PRACTICE: SPIRALS AND COLOR

As you move, have a specific lens on naturally occurring spirals and color. What kinds of colors stand out as you witness and connect with trees, grasses, clouds, and birds around you? What elements on flowers, in ice, or in the sky have natural, fractal-like, spiral-like patterns? What branches are twisting and bending? Do you notice spiral-like, radial patterns in the wounds on trees where branches used to be? You might pick up a small stone, pinecone, leaf, or blade of grass. Pause and honor it. Notice colors within colors. Notice any circles, complex vein arrangements, layers, or twisting elements. Imagine how each natural object is made and formed over time. Do you see the thin spirals in grass? Are there patterns? As you deepen your attention to naturally occurring spirals and colors in front of you, be mindful of the unique, nonlinear, and beautiful colors living inside of you.

TO BE IN AWE

When I think of moments in my day where awe stops me in my tracks, I am mostly by foot.

It is the way the glimmer of dusk reaches through dangling leaves.

It is the way finches collect dried grasses for their nests.

It is the way an older couple carefully walks while holding hands.

It is the way a flowing stream calms a racing mind.

It is the way street art beckons for love and liberation.

It is the way waves crash into coastal rocks at high tide.

It is the way a baby being carried by their parents stares back into my eyes and smiles.

It is the way an owl looks through you when flying in your direction.

It is the way an apple tastes after pulling it off the tree.

It is the way lightning commands attention.

It is the way a butterfly softly flies with you along the path.

It is all of this and so much more.

You are all of this and so much more.

I invite you to move with me under a setting sun so we can seek beauty and curiosity together. I invite you to rest by the ocean with me so we can feel the waves dissolve our walls. I invite you to let go, create, and dream with me.

DEDICATED PRACTICE

Take some time to move with the practice below. Do you know the Indigenous tribal lands you are walking or rolling on? Learn from and honor them as you move. Listen to your body. Honor your needs. Honor the lived reality of all who walk or use a wheelchair as their primary form around you. Honor what will work for you, especially depending on your ability, community, and context. No rules. Only invitation.

---------- Brave Creativity ----------

This practice is centered on protecting intentional time for walking or rolling specifically to nourish creative thinking, feeling, connecting, and dreaming. I sometimes like to picture my moving body combing the air between the world as it is and the world that is possible.

Creativity Prep: Protect time to write down or identify one or a few specific blocks, barriers, projects, dreams, ideas, or passions that would benefit from moving with an invitation of "Brave Creativity." Your list could include social or political issues you are grappling with, relationships you are trying to navigate, ideas and programs related to your work, projects you dream about working on, anything. You might just list one or two things to leave plenty of room for what organically arises. Take this list with you!

Grounding: Before you begin your movement, take a couple of deep breaths, all the way in and all the way out. As you breathe in, imagine the air you inhale breaking up mental blocks and cognitive fog. As you breathe out, imagine that you are releasing tasks, heavy thoughts, or anything that might hinder new ideas and creative thought. Take another deep breath in. As you breathe in, picture your lungs, mind, and heart making more room for creativity. Slowly and gently release your breath. If you have time, repeat each of these breathing invitations. Before and during your breathing exercises, give yourself a couple minutes to roll and lightly stretch your ankles, shoulders, neck, arms, back, and hips. You are physically and energetically making more room in your muscles, tendons, and bones for creative process.

Early Movement: For the first twenty minutes, or for as long as it makes sense to you, I invite you to bring your attention to your breathing and your movement. Try not to get too close to your thoughts or list yet. Let them pass by. You don't need to erase them. Just picture them like passing clouds that you may or may not return to. Continue your movement while trying to connect to your body and all that is alive around you.

Somewhere within this twenty-minute time frame, try on the following breathing practice. You might pause your movement, perhaps under a nearby tree to focus on your breath.

Breathe deeply in: Brave

Breathe deeply out: Creativity

Repeat

Breathe deeply in: Courageous

Breathe deeply out: Imagination

Repeat

Breathe deeply in: World as it is

Breathe deeply out: World that's possible

Repeat

Repeat the entire sequence now and as often as you like throughout your walk.

As you begin to move from this breathing practice, invite wonder, curiosity, color, and beauty. Try to look up at the sky as often as you can. Notice the clouds in one setting and then look again to see how they have formed, moved, and shifted. Notice where tree branches started from the trunk and how they evolved over time. Trace their bending and growing. What kind of nourishment might they have needed to thrive, to adapt in the spaces where no branches existed before? Be with this. Move with it.

Ongoing Movement: From here, take out your list. Read one or all lines first quietly to yourself, and then a second time out loud. Allow the creative process to unfold. If you read all of them, notice which one wants to come forward. Be with it. Let it roll around in your mind so it can make its way to your heart, and eventually to your body. As you imagine this project, relationship, idea, or block, invite the natural world around you and your very movement to assist you. Be open to surprises. Invite self-compassion for wherever creativity meets you. It is different for all of us. Some of you might have creative sparks right away. For others, it might take weeks or months to tangibly feel creative sparks. Honor your bravery for protecting this time. Honor your bravery for what these sparks might ask of you. You are not trying to solve or fix anything. You are making more room for creative process.

Timing and Location: Take at least thirty to forty minutes. Try your best not to be rushed. If you only have thirty minutes, keep your route small and perhaps in loops. It is extra helpful to be unhurried. Your location can truly be anywhere. For more room and space, you might try to move in places where there is less noise, fewer barriers, and more nature. Seek parks, valley trails, or even large plazas where you have plenty of access to air and sky. I also highly recommend doing this practice during a rising and setting sun.

TREES STREAMS & SKY

SEE US — HEAL US — GUIDE US

10

WALKING AS PRESENCE

SHE WAS A PORTAL

I will never forget the way it felt. Hundreds of them. I was surrounded. Each with their own unique steps and paths, but entirely together. This moment will be with me forever.

I was just arriving to the village of Portomarín. My father was a couple of hours behind me. We had four more days by foot to reach Santiago de Compostela. For the past twenty-six days, we had been walking the medieval Camino Frances pilgrim path in Spain.

I started making my way across the new bridge (Ponte Nova de Portomarín). It towered high above the Minho River and the old Portomarín ruins. The old village of Portomarín flooded in the 1960s. The new Portomarín was reconstructed, higher up in the mountains. As I moved along the bridge, the rail for pedestrians was especially low. Exposure to this lush expanse pushed my stomach into my chest. My breathing deepened. My eyes widened. I loved and relished the exposure of it all. I wanted to drink all of what I was seeing. I had to go explore the old ruins below.

Throughout our Camino, we walked alongside people from all over the world on a mix of ancient gravel roads, dirt paths, and streets.

Pilgrim villages, towns, and cities dotted the route every two to four miles. Rolling hills. Flowing streams. Wondrous trees. Unhurried time. My father and I would walk together for the first three miles and then decide where we would meet or finish along the way. My Father, David Milton Cox Stalls, played in three Super Bowls, founded an award-winning widely respected urban youth center in Denver called The Spot, fiercely loves his children and grandchildren, and so much more. He has inspired me from day one, and I will never begin to thank the stars enough for having him as my father and friend. I still cherish all the simple moments shared in those early morning walking hours. Always with a rising sun. Quietly moving with a cool breeze. Long stretches without words. Each step. Each laugh. Each story. Each blister. Each warm café con leche before we parted.

We were walking in September 2012 and water levels were low. I dropped off my things at the *albergue* (pilgrim hostel). I turned back toward the bridge and found some rugged stone stairs. Since it was low, I had to crawl and climb my way down through mud and tall grass.

I ventured out into the valley and already knew the spot that was calling to me. It was a tall and broken corner wall structure. Large weathered stones were mostly covered when the river was full. I climbed up to the top. It felt like I was all alone. I was in another world. The new bridge towered above me. I pulled out my journal to reflect on the day and sketch my surroundings.

As I began sketching, I noticed that something was coming toward me on the horizon. It resembled forming waves in the ocean as they make their way to the shore. I rubbed my eyes and put down my journal. My feet were now dangling on the corner of the old wall. Now I see it. An enormous herd of sheep were making their way across the river valley.

I relaxed my arms and calmed my gaze. My vantage point, high up on the wall, was incredible. While it may have only been ten minutes, it felt like hours for them to arrive.

Some would wander off and climb the old walls. Some stopped to eat grass. Most were bumping into one another and moving along. The sounds. The bells. The bleating cries. As they began to surround the old building I was sitting on, a couple of them tried to climb up. Every inch of bright green grass was now covered by a chorus of wooly gray-and-white bodies. It almost felt like I was being carried by the herd, stone wall and all. The stones rumbled underneath me as they moved.

I kept wondering who or what was guiding this massive herd. There were no humans in sight. No trucks. No horses. As I peered around the edges of this ocean of sheep, my eyes and heart widened when I saw two huge Pyrenean mastiffs combing the entire herd. I had never seen anything like it. Two dogs guiding hundreds of sheep. They were doing what they were made to do: nurturing and protecting the herd. I felt compelled to meet them, to move with them, if they would have me.

I took a deep breath. As soon as I started making my way down, I felt and noticed that the dogs were watching my every move. One was way in front and the other was well behind. I softly landed. I tried so hard to be as gentle as possible. As soon as my feet hit the ground, the dog in the front perked its head all the way up, signaling the one in the back, who was closer.

As I started to slowly move, surrounded by stumbling sheep, the dog from the back forced her way through the tightly packed herd. Her face was fierce. The flowing long white hair. The size of her frame. The confidence. The galaxy inside of and around her. The stare. Time stopped. She came right up to me. Her eyes never left mine. She had no other purpose but to protect the herd.

I felt that my capacity to be present and humble was a life-or-death situation. It was exhilarating and terrifying. I have never in my life felt this way before. Everything in the background began to fade away. She was a portal. Her gaze and face were focused and sharp. I was being scanned, on the inside and out, by a lineage of mastiffs dating back hundreds of years. Could I be trusted? What was my intention?

I knew that leaning down to pet her was not an option. As someone who has only really known domestic pet dogs, that was my default. I knew I needed to keep my hands to myself. I needed her approval and permission to take one more step. I remained completely still. I tried to source humility and patience, both in my heart and posture, as much as I could. I breathed deep and transitioned from looking into her eyes, looking up at the sky, and closing my eyes, constantly checking in on my intentions.

She smelled my legs and circled me several times. In a matter of moments, moments that felt like an eternity, she slowly nudged my leg with her nose and started slowly walking forward. It felt like I was given permission to at least begin moving. I wasn't sure, so I was extra gentle with each step.

After a couple of minutes, she turned her head up toward mine. I felt a shift. Her eyes communicated kindness and ease.

I slowly, very slowly, started walking forward. As soon as I did, she came even closer to my side, brushing my right leg with her large white fur with every step. It was as if the rhythm of our movement was the final test. The large bridge was now directly above us, and I noticed that the other dog in the front was periodically looking back, exchanging eye contact with her. Could I continue to be humble and present? Could I continue checking in with my intentions? Would I know when or if I was being asked to leave?

We continued to slowly move. A few more minutes went by. She was beginning to trust me. She moved about a foot away, but still very much at my side. Tears began to flow. I was smiling and weeping in surrender and awe. Nothing else mattered. The fog in my eyes and heart began to clear, and I was able to more fully see the hundreds of sheep surrounding us again.

After several more minutes, she paused. She looked up at me with calmness and warmth. That face. Those eyes. I was released.

I earned her trust. She slowly walked away toward the back. She began nudging some of the sheep who had wandered away. At that moment, the other dog in the front did the same. There I was. I was one of the many.

I walked with this community of angels for another thirty minutes. When I felt it was time leave, I stopped and relaxed my arms. I clasped my hands together and looked for the two dogs. They both noticed that I had stopped right away and perked up their heads. They knew. I knew that they knew. I waved and I smiled. Tears rushed.

As I made my way back to the bridge, I placed my hand on my heart. My whole being was full. I will never, ever forget them. This exchange tapped into every ache I have ever had about the way I longed for life to be—with myself, with other humans, with animals, and with the natural world around me.

INTEGRATION PRACTICE:
FLOWING WATER

As soon as I stepped foot on the tall bridge looming over the beautiful Minho River and its surrounding valley, I knew I had to venture down into it. For years I have found rivers, creeks, canals, small streams, and the ecosystems that surround them to be incredible places for rest, reflection, and presence. Protect some time next to a flowing water source near you. Bring a blanket, a light fold-up chair, or a small tarp in case the ground is wet. I recommend getting as close as you can to the water. You might try taking your shoes and socks off to place your feet in. Once you find a place to rest by flowing water, take several deep breaths. Ease into your breathing. Invite the water to see you, to honor what flows and moves on the inside, and perhaps to help carry things you want to release. Make time to *be with the water* itself. Allow the water to calm your mind, inspire your heart, and nourish your journey.

While I was seeking a moment of sketching, reflection, and presence on the old ruins, presence emerged and unfolded in unpredictable ways. It wasn't scheduled or performed. It flowed beneath me, the herd of sheep, and two wise shepherds. Slowly walking in this way kept the gifts of presence, of this great flow, close.

INVITATION TO BE

Calm, unhurried movement unquestionably helped me nurture trust with the two Pyrenean mastiffs. Moving by foot or wheelchair can more naturally help us pause, open, notice, and reflect on any number of details, questions, and surprises living within us and around us. It can also help us just be with what is. Sometimes we just need to move without anything new or fantastic or especially revealing.

INTEGRATION PRACTICE:
DEEP BREATHING

Starting, pausing in between, and closing my movement to take deep breaths always helps me to "be," even if just for a moment. Try to relax all the thoughts stirring in your mind. Begin to breathe a little deeper than what you are used to. As you breathe, imagine the air flowing down from your mind to your heart, and into your body. Simply concentrate on your breath. Slow and long breaths. Deeply in. Slowly out. Deeply in. Slowly out. Try planting both feet on the ground; perhaps open your palms to the sky. Try to release the stress you are carrying. As you invite deeper breaths, imagine the bronchi in your lungs like branches of reaching trees. Imagine each of the tiny bronchioles reaching, farther and farther, for more nourishment. Be with this practice, repeating deep breaths, for as long as you need. Notice what you are present to. Notice what starts to open in your mind and heart.

When we default to walking or rolling in a hurried fashion, which is real and raw for so many who depend on it for transportation, we maintain a state of bypassing what lives inside us and around us. Speeding things up and going from one thing to the next has been manufactured to be forward progress. So much gets lost when giving ourselves over to autopilot. As an athlete growing up, I can appreciate the thrill of speed, and the purpose of seeking it. That said, I have also become profoundly connected to the gifts, medicine, and wisdom of slowing down.

I don't need to produce anything. I don't need to solve anything. I don't need to prove anything. I don't need to perform anything. Just breathe. Just be.

MEDITATIVE MOVEMENT

In *Planetwalker,* Dr. John Francis (2009, 36) writes, "As you walk, look around, assess where you are, reflect on where you have been, and dream of where you are going. Every moment of the present contains the seeds of opportunity for change. Your life is an adventure. Live it fully."

Be with each of these invitations from Dr. Francis. Notice how they make you feel. Write them down and take them with you on your next walk or roll. Read them gently out loud as you move.

Meditation practices that involve stillness are incredibly good for me. I feel lighter, more at ease, and spacious in my body, mind, and heart. I also suck at them. I live most of my life constantly in motion and have always been a diehard under-the-table leg shaker. While I need and greatly benefit from times of stillness, it always feels like an uphill struggle.

My most natural form of connecting to a meditative state is (no surprise!) through unhurried, attentive, and patient movement. Stillness more naturally shows up for me in moments when I pause my movement to peer into a flower or a trickling stream. My moving body messages my mind, heart, and spirit, and stillness organically arrives with less pressure. It just happens. Sometimes it shows up in multiple five-minute increments along my commute. Sometimes it can last for hours on longer full-day walking experiences. Moving with meditative presence has profoundly helped ground me, calm me, and center any anxiety or stress I carry.

While I wouldn't necessarily say I'm a meditation teacher, I do really enjoy hosting and inviting meditative movement experiences. Most of the gatherings or practices I host don't come with too much programming or planning. I will usually spend a good amount of time scouting (prewalking) the route to make notes on access and safety. I will also use this time to see, feel, and listen to the elements and gifts around me: creeks, trees, flowers, birds, public art, stones, shade. There is already so much out in the world and deep within us that wants to guide, ground, and nourish our journey. That's what I love. It is not about me having answers or knowing the way. It is always about nurturing what intrinsically lives and arises within and around.

A beautiful friend of mine who recently transitioned from this life, Gina Mammano, wrote the book *Camino Divina,* in which she offers this beautiful invitation around the topic of walking meditation:

> It takes many forms, this "divine way" of walking. And there are many reasons people of all sorts meditatively walk. Some do it for clarity, abandoning the gush and rush of everyday life, hoping to replace it for a while with chaos, zephyrs, and winds of change. Others do it for reflection, a chance to reenter the motion pictures of their minds in order to recreate coherent story lines and begin new ones. Some seek self-forgiveness— the shoulders of granite above them and the arms of rivers below them holding a space for pain and transformation. Some look for internal healing from a past or a present rife with question marks, dancing and prodding them to engage the mystery, then allowing for the sweet surrender of self-care and solace. Others want understanding. An openness to the cosmos. Connection (Mammano 2016, xix).

Allow any ideas of right or wrong to gently fall from your shoulders as you move. Be patient with how you experiment and invite this in. Let self-compassion find you along the way. If you notice that your anxiety or stress isn't slowing down with you, return to your breath. Speak to your journey with patience and courage. Keep trying. Meditative movement brings together the inner and outer world. It invites us into the crashing waves and calm streams within us and around us.

INTEGRATION PRACTICE:
DISTINCT SOUNDS*

One way that helps me connect to a more meditative stance as I move is to intentionally invite the distinct and sometimes subtle sounds that exist around me. Before you move with this intention, take a couple of deep breaths. Ask that the sounds of the world around you reveal themselves to you. You might find that writing down some of the following sound examples will help support your practice.

- Your own feet walking or wheels rolling on various surfaces: gravel, grass, pavement
- Calls and songs of birds, katydids, and crickets
- Blowing, swirling wind around you or in the trees
- Your own breath inhaling and exhaling
- People talking and children playing
- Trains, airplanes, and sirens

---

* If you are hearing impaired, or if you want to adapt the practice, shift your focus to touch. Notice and reflect on the way textures feel: tree bark, a brick wall, leaves, a street pole, flowing water, rocks, sand, and so on.

- Rushing, trickling, and flowing water: rivers, creeks, gutters, canals, streams
- Squirrels, chipmunks, and other critters scurrying, chasing, or climbing

As you try to be present to a particular sound, take pause and allow extra time to let it move in and through you. Notice how you feel and what comes up when you hear it. Notice how these sounds connect to themes of collective movement—that even in hard and heavy times, we are all profoundly, cosmically in motion.

CATCHING UP WITH OURSELVES

Throughout any given day, there are storms of emotions and energies that move through us. With so much working to take hold of our attention, time, and resources, how we invite practices that ground and care for what we carry inside of us is critical. I see mindfulness, contemplation, prayer, meditation, and presence exercises as necessary tools that can help us nurture our wild and unique life journey.

Protecting time to invite presence, even if just for five minutes, can help us honor and witness what is real. In doing this, we give less power to what is ungrounded and fleeting. It is also important to name that reflection on our inner journey is complex and not always something we can just "turn on." Presence with oneself and with what surrounds us is whimsical and nonlinear. It swirls and bends. It isn't a switch or a button. I always turn to nature when I want to rest and be compassionately seen. Experimenting with meaningful practices and rituals has profoundly helped me catch up with all that swirls in and around me.

INTEGRATION PRACTICE:
INTENTION STONES

As pilgrims near the end of their Camino de Santiago journey, many will stop at a site called Cruz de Ferro, where they offer stones and gifts of intention, prayer, and remembrance. As you begin your movement, pick up one or several small stones. You could also pick up fallen acorns, pinecones, or wood pieces. Consider naming your pieces in representation of the intention you want them to embody. This could be an emotional or situational weight or essence: a memory; a specific fear; hardships; burdens; a loved one; Spirit, Great Mystery, God, or Goddess; ancestors; who I dream to be; who I really am; who I tried to be for others; wounds; dreams; a reminder to breathe.

As you move, you might have your stones in your hand to bring them closer to your senses and situation. You might pause to lay down the stone as a form of honoring your intention. You might throw or launch your stone into a lake or field as a form of honoring hurt, anger, or strength, or to release unwanted weight. You might hold onto your stones for days, for years, or forever. It all belongs. Allow your stones to be compassionate invitations of presence that embody the unique and tender intentions you give them.

Back to our breathing. Back to our body. Back to a blossoming flower and a rising sun. Back to unhurried movement with all that we are, as we are.

DEDICATED PRACTICE

Take some time to move with the practice below. Do you know the Indigenous tribal lands you are walking or rolling on? Learn from and honor them as you move. Listen to your body. Honor your needs. Honor the lived reality of all who walk or use a wheelchair as their primary form around you. Honor what will work for you, especially depending on your ability, community, and context. No rules. Only invitation.

―――――――――― Unhurried Witness ――――――――――

Practice Context: This invitation is inspired by a style of contemplative practices called *Lectio Divina* (Divine Reading) and *Visio Divina* (Divine Seeing). They are popular in various spiritual, Christian and mystical, and nonreligious traditions where you move through a process of slowly and more intentionally honoring and listening to the wisdom of words and visuals.

Grounding and Early Movement: Start with a few deep breaths. Check in with your body by stretching and lightly warming up. Notice your thoughts and then try to release them. It's okay if they come back. They surely will. Continue to notice them and release them. Begin to slowly move. As you move, notice your pace. Be unhurried. Rest into gentle, patient, and spacious movement. Calmly witness your surroundings as you go.

Finding Your Element, Piece, or Natural Object: As you continue your movement, begin openly listening with your eyes and heart for a natural object, element, public art piece, mural, or anything that might be seeking more of your time, attention, and reflection. Be patient and curious. Maybe you are drawn to a specific tree. From there, you might feel guided to sit under it. Maybe you are drawn to sit next to a large sculpture in the distance. Maybe a pile of fallen bright-red leaves is calling. From there, you might be invited to peer into the sculpture itself, into a ladybug slowly walking near it, into a specific branch in the tree, or into a bird's nest just above it. Allow these natural objects or elements to draw you in. As you are drawn in, try to choose an art piece, natural object, or vibration that you can form a deeper and more intimate connection with.

Once you have your piece, object, or element, invite the four stages below. Read aloud, to yourself, or as prerecorded audio. Timing notes are merely suggestions. Make it yours.

Stage 1: Witness (four minutes or more): As you begin to look into your element or connection, take a few moments to open your heart and mind. Allow your eyes to simply notice the object or specific element. Take your time. Invite feelings and thoughts to come to you as you take in forms, figures, colors, lines, textures, and shapes within your chosen piece. What does it look like or remind you of? What do you find yourself drawn to? What are your initial thoughts? What feelings arise?

In this initial stage, simply notice these responses. Try not to focus on any one response. Try not to understand them. Calmly ground your attention, and try to stay open to the image and the practice.

Move and Breathe (two minutes or more): Pause and close your eyes. Take one or two deep breaths. Honor what you noticed. You might walk or move to invite flow and space. Feel your feet. Feel the wind. Move with what you saw. After a few minutes, return to the image, perhaps from a different angle.

Stage 2: Meditate (four minutes or more): As you return, slowly open your eyes, and with an open heart and mind, gravitate to a specific section in the image or element. New thoughts, new meanings, new feelings, and new reactions may arise. Your initial impressions may expand and deepen. Explore more fully what is coming to you, and the feelings associated with this specific area in the object, element, or image. Be aware of any preconceived ideas you might bring. No matter what your responses are—wonder, joy, dread, blankness, anger, grief, inspiration, complexity—be with them. You are not trying to solve anything. Simply witness them.

Move and Breathe (two minutes or more): Pause and close your eyes. Take one or two deep breaths. You might walk or move around near your image, perhaps this time in a different direction or pattern. Notice how any responses and details move with you. After a few minutes, return to the image, perhaps from a different angle.

Stage 3: Invitation (four minutes or more): As you return, open yourself up to what the specific area within the image, or the image as a whole, might be trying to reveal to you. Is there something that it might be saying or wanting to make known? What might this object, art piece, or element be inviting? Listen for it. Be with it. Become aware of thoughts, desires, and meanings that arise and how they might be connected to your life. Are there sounds? Are there textures? Invite deeper listening and touch. Be mindful of how you find yourself wanting to respond to what you are experiencing.

Move and Breathe (two minutes or more): Pause and close your eyes. Take one or two deep breaths. You might walk or move. Notice what you are feeling. Moving and being. After two minutes, return to the image, perhaps from a different angle.

Stage 4: Embody (four minutes or more): As you return, be mindful of the insights you want to remember. Comb through the messages, details, reactions, and invitations offered from this connection. As you continue peering into the image, consider any unique actions you might want to take, wisdom you hope to absorb more fully, or any feelings or thoughts you wish to express with others or in writing. Be with these things. Honor them. Seek integration. Bring your practice to a close with a couple of deep breaths and gratitude.

Time: Spend at least twenty to thirty minutes.

Location: Do it anywhere. Commercial streets, a nature trail, the front yard, an alley, a parking lot, anywhere. This is about being present with wherever this invitation finds you. You might consider doing it in multiple locations to draw from a variety of scenarios.

11

WALKING AS RITE OF PASSAGE

FIRST STEPS

I looked long and hard at the Atlantic Ocean on that first day, March 1, 2010. Each wave carried all my memories and dreams. My eyes welled up with tears. Everything I had suppressed for so long began to dance in front of me. The sand was cool but welcoming. The sky was overcast with a calm late-winter breeze. The sound of rolling and crashing water soothed my fear. A few friends, family, and supporters stood in the distance holding their own stories of curiosity and wonder.

I was swirling.

I was elated.

I was terrified.

Would I make it a week?

Would I survive?

Would Kanoa survive?

Who would help me along the way?

What dangerous situations would I encounter?

What would I see and experience that might change me forever?

Do I have what it takes to survive?

Do I have what it takes to love who I am?

These questions and so many more kept rushing around the ache to just start. I had done my best to plan and prepare. It was now up to nature, to Spirit, to the people in my midst, and to the growing edges of strength inside of me.

Kanoa and I started walking. As I turned away from my starting point, taking my first steps west, I choked up with tears and excitement, as I had honored a very deep and visceral cry to live out a new story for how I see myself, how I see others, and how I connect with the land around me.

I still remember how it felt to smash my microwave, knee snap my laptop, strip naked, light candles, and play the guitar while bawling my eyes out in the fall of 2007 after watching the movie *Into the Wild,* the story of Chris McCandless. A couple of months later, I stumbled upon *A Walk Across America* by Peter Jenkins at an Auraria Campus Library book sale. I skipped all my classes and read it cover-to-cover in two days. That was the beginning.

"I can do this.

"We can do this.

"One step at a time.

"One sunset at a time."

I kept saying this to myself over and over as we got farther away from the shore. I was shedding stories that no longer serve me. I was growing new skin and diving into canyons of risk and growth.

As a twenty-seven-year-old man on the outside, I still felt young and ill-equipped on the inside. I had never done anything like this before. I didn't camp much growing up. I never went on long multi-day hikes or backpacking trips. It was me, Kanoa, and my new over-stuffed, ninety-pound home on my back.

I was about an hour into the walk and was standing on a small dirt hill at an intersection with no sidewalks. It was funny to me that I had to walk down the dirt hill, balancing on the muddy slope, to just barely get to the pedestrian crossing button. This was my first of what would soon be thousands of examples where pedestrians and people who use wheelchairs have been almost entirely left out of land development and transportation planning.

Cars lined up at the intersection. I looked at the drivers, smiled, and offered a few awkward waves. While I was able to get a few smiles and waves in return, I also got several shakes of the head, a few middle fingers, and several eye rolls. I remember how I immediately tucked into my shell, avoided eye contact, and began feeling and feeding the same toxic voices that have tried to wipe out my truths for as long as I can remember. I wanted to deeply believe in myself, to feel strong, and more than anything, to feel capable. I wanted my love of self to blaze past the stares, middle fingers, and eye rolls.

It was some of the best practice. It still is. Standing there at intersections. Waiting to cross, clutching my dignity as judgments are fired my way through lanes of idling cars. As a kid, I fantasized about how I would disappear and escape all the teasing I received as a sensitive and artistic new student in twelve different schools. It would often resemble wings that would rip through the skin on my back, opening on command. I would soar above and beyond all the fear, anger, and shame of it all. Maybe this is why most of my dreams involve the option to fly.

We kept moving. I could already feel the early growth of new roots forming in my feet and heart. As we got farther and farther away, I felt my spirit and body shedding and releasing what it no longer needed. I knew, right then, that this would be a slow, painful, and liberating journey of cutting artificial strings while welcoming a more natural source of wisdom that I could trust with everything in me.

I was leaving so many ideas and possessions behind. I gave myself away to the wisdom of nature, my own limitations, endless unknowns, and so much more. This was a walk into the world and all its color, into the hearts of strangers and future friends, and into the depths of transformation inside my unsettled soul. It was only day 1, and I had never felt such strong symbiotic movement between my physical body and inner spirit. The drums that circled in my stomach were loud and clear. I was at the mercy of all that was out of my control. I was ready to feel alive.

THE ACHING EDGE

Rev. Dr. Howard Thurman writes:

> There is something in every one of you that waits, listens for the sound of the genuine in yourself, and if you cannot hear it, you will never find whatever it is for which you are searching.... You are the only you that has ever lived; your idiom is the only idiom of its kind in all of existence, and if you cannot hear the sound of the genuine in you, you will all of your life spend your days on the ends of strings that somebody else pulls.

Reflect on this reading. Tremble with it. Write it down. Shut the book and move with it. How might you hear the sound of the genuine in you? What might need to shift, move, or be rattled to make more room for hearing this sound? How would you begin to describe the strings in your life that others pull?

As we attempt to seek and hear our own genuine sound, what edges exist inside us and around us? Where are there voids, chasms, and canyons? I often refer to these "aching edges" as places and spaces where we feel we are too frightened to go. They are places that test us, push us, and even threaten us. Perhaps we go there often to tend to them, listen to them, and learn from them. Perhaps we only journey there when necessary, or when nearly forced by external circumstances. Or, perhaps, we do everything imaginable, understandably, to stay as far away as we can. All of this belongs. It is endlessly nonlinear, and you are where you are.

Rite of passage exploration and movement can be a wondrous realm of courage, suffering, severing, and triumph to begin breaking through the heaviness of tired and toxic ways. It will root you into your own sense of agency and dignity. A rite of passage journey must be unique to you. Your skin. Your aches. Your fires. Your experiences. They will not be mine, or anyone else's.

Walking or rolling is a wondrous field of experimentation in rite of passage exploration. Our landscapes around us long to mirror more openly the landscapes within us. It takes us humbly away from most walls and artificial or monitored time. We can't as easily hide from storms and animals. We can't as easily avoid people. We can't as easily avoid what surfaces from the inside. Experiences like this invite us to see and feel how we are more intrinsically woven with birds, thunder, sunsets, one another, and the stars.

I personally believe that if we want to feel truly alive in this life, if we want to survive as a species, and if we seek to wake up to our intuition, we need to go to these aching edges. I am inviting you into your own fire, knowing that somewhere in the storm, your fire touches mine and mine touches yours. You are never alone, and no one will hear your genuine sound for you.

YOUR OWN EDGES

There are no right or wrong ways to move into a rite of passage experience, and there are numerous traditions, cultures, and rooted practices that honor this significant invitation far beyond what I have shared here. If you seek traditions that are not from your own culture or lineage, avoid appropriation of any kind and seek relationship, blessing, and guidance from those who are from those traditions. Embody a spirit of humility, spaciousness, and respect.

Movement experiences that require discernment and risk around where to sleep, what path to take next, where to find food, and how to overcome fear have helped ground my life in ways I never thought possible. I continue to embody long-distance walking experiences as a way of seeking and tending to my own edges. For me, moving through mixed environments that combine the wild and natural with the paved and developed offer a sense of wholeness, honesty, and tension that I deeply trust. There is something so important to me about not separating the two. I feel like I can integrate what I learn and feel in the wilderness with what I learn and feel on the small highway. This complex tension helps me not to abandon industrial devastation while connecting with the gifts of natural beauty.

INTEGRATION PRACTICE:
SCREAMS, HOWLS, AND TEARS

We have too much telling us and cornering us to cover up what is actually happening inside of us. Keep it tidy. Keep it neat. Keep it clean. We desperately need nurturing, raw, and soulful ways to express our deep fears, anger, grief, shame, joy, pain, generational trauma, and desires. When we move, we physiologically invite and allow these aches to surface more organically and naturally. As you move, seek out moments and spaces that can hold and witness your screams, howls, shouts, groans, tears, dancing, and trembling. It might be on top of a hill or mountain. It might be into the raging rapids of a river. It might be into the winds of a storm. It might be into the depths of a night sky. It might be under a large mature tree. There is no need to have words for anything that you offer. I also recommend trying this with someone you trust and love. It is a powerful, tender, and courageous act to be witnessed. It also invites shared communal release. Sometimes all we have are our messy, wordless aches.

Movement experiences like this don't need to be long-distance. They can be right out your front door and broken up into any number of smaller segments. They must honor your body and physical and environmental limits as they are. Your unique edges are radical, wild, and complex. Invite them. Listen to them. Honor and stretch them. Starting on that trail, rural road, suburban cul-de-sac, beach, or small highway and walking or rolling for days at a time is absolutely unsafe.* In many ways, it needs to be. Create backup plans and invite others to join you. Appoint a team of volunteers to help coordinate home-stays and support vans.

As soon as you begin, the rawness of it all will break you, surprise you, and liberate you in plenty. Growing a new and more grounded root system requires that you break free from the weight of the old. Release all expectations to the wind, stop when you need to stop, and love yourself fiercely.

SHEDDING WHAT NO LONGER SERVES US

Accountability to unstructured, unhurried time is one of the main reasons I trust one-to-three-miles-per-hour human movement as a form of rite of passage. If I am only tearing off what no longer serves me, which is often necessary, then the old skin or story leaves a gaping wound that needs time to heal. I always reference trees. Sometimes certain branches need to break off so new energy can grow and reach in new places. New growth can take longer because significant energy is needed to heal the break. What kinds of experiences and practices can allow things to shed or fall away because we take the time to face them, learn from them, move with them, and select them for extinction? I love juniper trees. They embody all of these invitations. Next time you see one, pause to notice their constant state of shedding, their wide range of deep colors, and all the breaking, bending, twisting, and adapting living in their branches.

---

* If you are Black, LGBTQIA2S+, a person of color, a person with a disability, a woman, an older adult, or another minority, this kind of experience needs to be met with even greater care. There are people in the world who identify with each of the identity descriptions I have named who have taken long, multiday, and multiple-month walking and rolling experiences. Seek their advice and guidance.

I want you to invite the relationship of moving in the outside world with our invisible microscopic skin flakes. When we are sitting in stuffy indoor environments, these skin cells stick, stack, and clump together on and all around us. We may not see it, but how might piles of dead skin impact feelings of stiffness in our thoughts and hearts? Imagine what it would be like to see all the dead skin fall, flake, and fly off our shoulders, backs, arms, head, and legs as we move. I love thinking of the wind returning them to the dirt.

In what ways are you protecting time to shed stories that no longer serve you? Moving in the outside world helps us shed deadweight, dead ideas, and dead skin. Imagine what kind of shedding can take place when moving for days, weeks, or months at a time.

INTEGRATION PRACTICE:
SHELLS, COCOONS, AND FALLEN BRANCHES

There is so much in the natural world that teaches on the role of shedding, decay, releasing deadweight, and transformation. As you move, be extra mindful to notice all the dead skin left from trees, plants, insects, and critters around you. Pick up various collections of fallen bark, leaves, shells, and sticks as you go. Honor the details. Try to really feel what a caterpillar went through to transform into a butterfly. You might also look for pieces that are starting to peel off but remain attached to their source. What kind of wind, or jolt, or storm might be needed to release or free up what is to come? As a queer person, nature's way of communicating transformation and adaptation offers me endless permission to release, shed, express, heal, and thrive the way I am made to. As you move, reflect on your unique shedding journey and what might need to break, bend, or be released to make room for new growth.

ACHES OF A WITNESS: WALKING FORT COLLINS TO PUEBLO

A dear friend of mine, Naveed Heydari, shares about how rite of passage–inspired walking practice impacted him while moving along a custom two-hundred-mile walking route I put together (see hand-drawn maps on the Intrinsic Paths website, www.intrinsicpaths.com) from Fort Collins to Pueblo, Colorado.

> I am Naveed Heydari, a half-Ecuadorean, half-Persian, American-born queer man. The mantra, "Do I have what it takes?" shook my body and tenderized my heart. In a video reflection connected to this practice, Jonathon was walking on a seemingly never-ending rural dirt road lined with cholla cacti as far as the eye could see. Months later, I would be walking across that same terrain on my final day into Pueblo, Colorado, and feeling confident that not only "I have what it takes," but also, "I have more than what it takes. I have always had what it takes. If it is important to me, I have what it takes." Moreover, "I have what it takes to dismantle the untruths that live within me and let my own inner truth emerge from the rubble."

> I was (am) blessed with my relationship to the mountains that accompanied my every step.

> I was (am) blessed with the flowing water in the many creeks at my side.

> I was (am) blessed by the thousands of trees that I made contact with through my eyes, hands, and heart.

> I was (am) blessed by the ground and the earth that opened my soles and my soul to their healing presence.

> I was (am) blessed with the morning colors of the sunrise and the evening backdrop of the sunset.

> One of my biggest transformations on this walk was in relationship to pain, discomfort, and resilience. After a couple of days, I was very concerned about my knees and lower back. I was also convinced that I would get sick on several occasions, especially the day I crossed the freezing river and couldn't feel my feet, or

the day I walked ten hours in a blizzard. I could hear my grandma's voice: *"Te vas a enfermar!"* (You're going to get sick!)

The truth is, I have never slept better or felt better in my life. I didn't get sick once and all my joints responded very well to walking hundreds of miles. The walk was an incredibly healing experience, a cleansing container to flush my body and mind of stories that were outdated. My body craves to be used, to be outside in challenging conditions, to feel cold at times, and to feel exposed. My body is incredibly resilient and wants to be taken to the edges of what society traditionally defines as discomfort. In our overculture that avoids discomfort or pain at all costs, it was an incredibly liberating act to choose to move into pain and find out what is on the other side.

On the other side, I found compassion and communion. I kept walking when my knee hurt, but I did so with compassion by moving fewer miles, taking more breaks, and leaving heavy items behind at a friend's place. On the final day of my journey, I walked thirty-plus miles with a full pack, and my knees felt great. On the many days when my heart was heavy, I found communion with the many parts of me that I neglected for so long by giving them the space to be witnessed, to be held.

My body is my ally. My pain is a friend. I am sick and in pain most often when my life choices are not aligned with my truths and inner compass. I walked more than 220 miles and I did it in a way that was just for me: listening to my needs, centering my desires, focusing my truths. The result was that my body, mind, and spirit responded with a healthier, stronger, and more resilient version of me.

The most challenging aspect of this walk was realizing how much I have internalized belief systems and paradigms that harm me, stories and constructs that I don't actually want to believe in. Voices like, "You are supposed to do it this way," or, "That's not how it should be done" were regular visitors. While the walk gave me so much permission to release these belief systems, the transformation was very messy and quite painful.

On the second morning of my journey, I was already feeling defeated. In the winter season of Colorado, I spent a cold, sleepless night with aching joints. Physically, I couldn't convince myself to get going. Finally, when I did pack up camp, I was flooded with all my internal stories scolding me for my late start. "See, this is proof that you are broken and defective. We knew you couldn't last more than a day." These stories weighed me down. They were in control. I collapsed numerous times this day, crying for long periods under train tracks, next to river banks, and on busy roads. I barely made it to the midway point of the day's planned route, and I felt crushed when I heard the voice again, poignant and charged: "I don't have what it takes."

I fell again, and maybe for the first time in my life, I let myself experience and bear witness to the fullness of this part of me. And something started to shift as I sobbed, shivering, on the cold pavement. The changes were slow but consistent. First, a stranger walked by and asked me in Spanish if I was unhoused and needed help. That small act meant the world to me. He walked with me for a mile in silence to the Loveland library. In the parking lot, a stranger inquired about my journey and offered me some cannabis for my aching joints.

Inside the library (thank goodness for free public spaces to rest and reset), I was able to reflect: "Wait—who says I have to follow the route as it is? Who says I must carry this amount of weight? Who says I must walk twenty miles a day? Who says I have to be in this much pain?"

My whole body and soul felt heavy when I realized that I was letting my subconscious beliefs about success and worthiness dictate my journey. And the same way they showed up in this walking trip, they have been showing up in my life.

It was time to alchemize the old stories into the new ones. It was time to break all the inner rules. It was time to do things my way. The next day, I got rid of half the weight in my backpack, and I walked that day's route in the opposite direction. With each successive day I felt lighter and lighter as I followed my inner guidance and truth. By the end of the fortnight, I thought

I would be needing lots of rest, but actually, the opposite was true. I had never felt more ready.

This walk was the most powerful rite of passage that I have ever experienced. On my final day, I awoke at 3 a.m. and knew that I had what it took. I was ready to complete my journey. January 2, 2019: It was the coldest and riskiest part of the trip for me. Like my ancestors, I prayed for the sun to come out that day. I believed that if I stopped walking, the sun wouldn't come out. Now, that's a transformation. I started the trip thinking I was not worthy and that nothing I did mattered, and on the final day I believed that I was essential to summon the sun for that day.

I am
radiant
non-linear
imperfect
& cosmic

When the sun peeked through the horizon, I stopped to take in the magical colors. I was on the same rural road lined with cholla cacti that Jonathon had traversed months before. I had done it. I had imbued the rite of passage with my unique and beautiful life energy. By making it my own, I proved to myself the truth all along: that I have what it takes to create meaningful and memorable experiences for myself; that I can trust in how I trust and love others, like Jonathon, as sacred mentors and guides; that I am worthy of life's pleasures.

My dear friends, you are worthy of designing rites of passages that are meaningful and relevant to you. You give us life when you choose life. Love and acceptance for wherever you are, however you show up.

DEDICATED PRACTICE

Take some time to move with the practice below. Do you know the Indigenous tribal lands you are walking or rolling on? Learn from and honor them as you move. Listen to your body. Honor your needs. Honor the lived reality of all who walk or use a wheelchair as their primary form around you. Honor what will work for you, especially depending on your ability, community, and context. No rules. Only invitation.

I Have What It Takes

There are no words for what it felt like to reach the halfway mark in Kansas, the Colorado River in Utah, the high desert in Nevada, and ultimately the sandy shores of the Pacific Ocean on November 13, 2010. Reaching the other coast across a wondrous rainbow of experiences is something my heart, body, and soul will never forget. I had family, friends, host families from the walk, and Kiva's staff join me on that final day. We had a hundred people walking to the ocean together. My 3,030-mile walking journey was an eruption of embodied learning and growing. When I neared the shore, I threw off the pack and ran with Kanoa at my side. I splashed into those West Coast waters knowing that I could forever touch and draw from this newly rooted relationship to ground. "I have what it takes" wasn't just an idea; it was now deeply embedded into my being. While I will always struggle, fall short, carry doubts, and deeply feel the pressure of a hurting world around me, I know my name, and I can feel my ground.

The dedicated practice for this theme is rooted in finding your unique path or route that invites your own growth edges. Your route or movement journey should feel a little daunting. Whether it is based on the duration, distance, or any one environment, there should be some level of trembling. For many, having support around you might be key to consider this practice. For others, it is shutting down all unhelpful voices and taking that first step or roll. You might organize a support team; you might not. You might have backup options and friends to call and check on you; you might not. Maybe this is a weekend or a month of walking or rolling to start. Maybe you just need to leave it all behind and go where the wind takes you. No timelines. No goals. All of it belongs.

If You Need a Plan: Needing a plan is understandable. When I walked across the United States, I sort of had a plan. I studied online maps, the American Discovery Trail, and the routes of others who had walked across the country. I ended up abandoning most of my plans within a week or so of the walk. Be you and honor the amount of structure you might crave or need to take those first steps. I would advise that you lean into a plan that avoids getting too detailed. If it is too detailed, then much of the magic and emergence gets stuck in meeting expectations. Try to focus your planning on what you will bring, what general direction you might go, support and safety networks, and most importantly, the day you will start.

Locations, Examples, Ideas: They're anywhere, everywhere. For many, having already existing routes, themes, and meaningful destinations can help structure, anchor, and ground a long-distance movement journey. For those that are considering this option, I have included a list of specific examples and broader ideas below to get the juices flowing:

- **Origin, ancestors, roots, and lineage:** This is a route, already existing or one that you create, that honors your ancestral past, heritage, or culture. Research and draw from your family origin story and seek places that can reveal, ground, and nourish your roots.

- **Popular or religious pilgrim paths:** These are ancient paths that people have taken for spiritual, religious, or ceremonial purposes. Examples could be the Camino de Santiago in Spain, the Chimayó pilgrimage route in New Mexico, the Hajj pilgrimage, Mount Kailash in Tibet, Kumano Kodo in Japan, and the Abraham Path in the Middle East. It is important to deeply honor and respect the local rooted culture of these pilgrimage experiences versus seeing them or experiencing them as a tourist. Move with integrity, relationship, and humility.

- **Migration, justice, and survival routes:** These are paths that various people or groups have taken when traveling by foot, horse, or other means for relocation, protest, survival, starting over, seasonal relocation, and remembrance. Examples could be the Selma to Montgomery, Alabama, civil rights route; the Old Spanish Trail from Santa Fe, New Mexico, to Southern California; the Trail of Tears forced displacement of Native Americans from the Southeastern United States; the Mormon Trail from Illinois to Utah; the March on Washington; the Pony Express route; and Standing Rock in North and South Dakota.

- **National Scenic Trails and statewide trails:** These are nationally or regionally funded and supported long-distance trail networks focused on preservation and public recreation. Not all trails are completely supported and mapped. Examples: Continental Divide Trail, Pacific Crest Trail, Appalachian Trail, Colorado Trail, American Discovery Trail, Florida Trail, Arizona Trail, Santa Fe Trail, Long Trail, Ala Kahakai Trail, Ice Age Trail, the East Coast Greenway, and others.

- **Thematic structure:** This involves creating custom routes that are designed to (a) tell a story of a city, a people, or landscape, or (b) embody a variety of beliefs, themes, chakras, signs, or inspirational invitations.

- **Proximity webs:** These are routes, paths, and landscapes that extend from where you live. Create several strings of smaller routes or one long one that circles, visits, and maps communities, villages, towns, and geographic destinations within a certain radius around your home or perhaps the place you grew up.

- **No structure at all:** See what shows up as you go. One step or roll at a time. An important reminder: this option exists and is very much alive.

Timing: Open and free. No limits. Tender and courageous. Into the horizon for as long as you are able, for as long as you can, for as long as you desire.

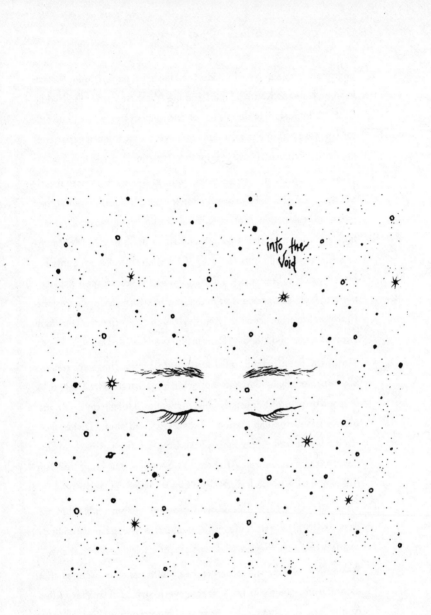

12

WALKING AS MYSTERY

A JELLYFISH IN THE SKY

We were winding down on day 188 after just walking up and over Sacramento Pass, which lies just west of Baker, Nevada, near Great Basin National Park, along highway 50, Nevada's branded "Loneliest Highway in America." Public land was all around us, and my friend Jolene came from Denver to walk with me for a few days. The landscapes here are otherworldly.

We set up our tents fifty feet off the road in a flat gravel area surrounded by wondrous blue sage. The smell, color, and feel of it all inspires every cell in my body. This valley stretches out between 2 of 314 mountain ranges across Nevada. My tent is within arm's reach of Jolene's, and we are finally lying down, staring up at the stars, and resting.

The night before, we stayed in a straw-bale birth dome. It belonged to an amazing family in an inspiring intentional living community. I admired how everyone rooted into simple, shared, and Earth-centered life practices. Before heading to bed, we stood outside with our host family, looking up at the stars. They warned us that mountain lions were out and that someone was attacked by one a couple of weeks back. They also shared that there was unusual activity above the pass and to keep our eyes open. When I first heard them say strange activity, I thought, "Um, ha, y'all are the strange activity."

Jolene shared with me that she was getting cold and may not have enough covering to keep her warm. I had an extra blanket in my custom cross-country walking Bob stroller. (Thank you, global walker Polly Letofsky!) I unzipped my tent and fumbled to get my blanket over to her. As I turned back into my tent, I saw a bright blazing image in the distance. It was the exact area where we had been guided to pay attention. I couldn't believe what I was seeing. I immediately scrambled my way out of the tent and started walking away from our camp toward what was floating in the sky.

As I started to make out what I was seeing—"Shit! No way. What in the actual ..."—I quickly disconnected from Jolene, our camp, my own body, and the walk. It was huge. Like, really huge, considering the perspective of where it appeared to be floating. It resembled a large jellyfish-like object hovering in the sky. It flashed and transitioned from bright green to bright orange, from bright orange to bright yellow. It expanded out and in, out and in, much like lungs with bright neon tentacles. The tentacles or spiraling strings flowed under and around it.

I rubbed my eyes several times.

"No way. Jonathon, you are officially losing it."

There it was. Still inflating and deflating. Still shifting colors. I shook my head and rubbed my eyes again.

"Wha-a-at! Impossible. Absolutely impossible."

I shook my head again. I rolled my shoulders. I did a summersault (not sure why) and proceeded with one more aggressive eye rub.

Still there. Everything.

It continued to float and slowly expand in and out. At this point, I gave in. Here it was. Here I was. I started to walk slowly toward it. It felt five to ten miles away, but it felt so close. I fell down on my knees. I began speaking to it:

"Take me with you.

"You can trust me.

"I've walked so many miles.

"We can learn so much from each other.

"Take. Me. With. You."

All the sci-fi movies. All the color. All the wonder.

I kept rubbing my eyes. "Am I making this up? Am I dreaming? No. This is very much real." The cosmic UFO is still here. I am very much here.

My arms are now up and out. I am unapologetically inviting this goddess alien ship to beam me up. One more minute passes by. It feels like an eternity. I can hear Jolene in the background asking what the hell is going on.

I later find out she thinks it's a mountain lion.

The next thing I know, the object gets brighter, and the color transitions speed up. It does a dramatic turn to the side and flies, with a spiral and a swirl, into the distance.

Gone. Completely gone.

"OMG. OMG. OMG."

I ran back to my tent and drew every little detail into my small journal. I asked everyone who crossed my path for days after if they had ever seen anything like it. No one had seen what I described. Jolene, of course, never saw it.

I see you, smirking. Y'all, the brightness, the aliveness, the colors. My experience witnessing this galactic jellyfish has and will impact my relationship to the wonder and wildness of the unknown for the rest of my days.

INTEGRATION PRACTICE:
HONORING THE NIGHT

In whatever ways make sense to you—meditative steps in your back yard, relaxed walking or rolling in a nearby park, moving with new and full moons, or strolling on quiet low-traffic streets—protect time to move your body under a night sky. As you move, try to be in your senses as much as possible. Listen. Feel. Look up and allow your eyes to get lost in the stars as often as you can. You might bring a towel or small blanket to find a spot to lie down. As you look up into the night sky, invite the theme "mystery" into your thoughts and heart. Be mindful of how the night invites you to exist in all that is unseen.

SO LONG, CERTAINTY

In the daytime, I will often close my eyes and push the palms of my hands up against them to limit any light peeking through. I did this a lot as a kid. I think it was another form of escape, trying to fly and travel the universe whenever I wanted. As my eyes are closed, I experience what looks and feels like blurry stars. I feel like I'm soaring with and beyond them. While my brain tries to explain to me that all those sparkly lights are just reflections and glares from when my eyes were open, I ignore it. It feels like an always available portal to cosmic wisdom.

When I walk, my relationship to the unknown is intimate and ever-present. The number of moments that surprise me, inspire me, and devastate me are uncountable as I make my way along-side a wide variety of urban streets, suburban cul-de-sacs, rural dirt roads, and river greenways. As I move, I rest, more and more, into the notion that if I am certain of anything at all, it is that I am uncertain. I know, in so many ways, that I truly do not know. This humbling and liberating truth often resembles the wind swirling in and around me. There is no clear beginning or end. It just is. As I am. As it is. As we are.

As you weave more intention into your movement, your relationship to the great void, the great chasm, and the cosmic unknown has the chance to expand in ways that open you, challenge you, and inspire you. No other practice, no individual teacher, no self-help program, no spiritual retreat has ever come close to the vibration of what a good long walk or roll can do for my spirit and my connection to the miracles and mysteries living deep inside me, deep inside others, and in my surroundings.

INTEGRATION PRACTICE:
AROUND THE BEND AND JUST AHEAD

Begin with a deep breathing practice. As you breathe, relax your mind, feel your body, and open your heart. Be mindful that as you invite deeper breaths, you also make more room to witness and connect with all the mysteries in and around you. What might greet me on the other side of the hill? Who might be sitting in the park benches today? If I were to strike up a conversation with someone waiting for the bus, what will I learn or see or feel? Will I see anyone on the other side of the building when I turn the corner? How will I feel when I make my way down from the bridge to touch the flowing water? How have the trees changed since the last time I was here? If you notice your mind jumping in with tasks and distractions, return to your breath. Continue inviting all that is unseen. Continue moving with all that reveals itself to you. If we adopt a practice of welcoming uncertainty on our walks, then we might be able to accept it more naturally in all areas of our lives.

FOLLOW THE FLUFFY TAIL

It was day 9. We arrived in the village of Piediluco on my birthday. I still remember the small path that took us out to the lake, right on the edge of the town. The sun was out. Families were out. There was a freely roaming sheepdog running around us for a bit. She had a significant limp in her back right leg. She wasn't in pain, and she moved like she had been limping that way for years.

My partner, Ben, and I were walking the Way of Saint Francis (Via Francigena di San Francesco) from Assisi to Rome in rural Italy in 2019. We were celebrating our one-year anniversary of being married. We have known each other for over sixteen years at the time of writing this book. He joined me for over five weeks on my cross-country walk. He also moved through his own Camino de Santiago experience in 2018.

Walking is a pillar for us. It helps us process, vent, celebrate, dream, and listen. We have gone through a lot together. Heavy things. Confusing things. Inspiring and wonderful things. We have split up and gotten back together six times. We have moved through, literally and metaphorically, plenty of thick fog together. I love him. I love us. I am endlessly grateful for all that we get to experience together when moving through the world in this way.

I kneeled to pet her. Ben kept his distance. He didn't grow up with dogs and had a couple of hard encounters with them when he was young. For him, all dogs, especially roaming ones, were suspect.

She stayed for a minute but had things to do. We were well used to free-range community dogs in many of the smaller villages. There was, though, something special about her. It didn't feel random. It was almost like she was checking in with us.

We were up early to start walking with the rising sun. As soon as we stepped out from our hotel, there she was. She was no more than twenty feet away, sprawled out, sleeping on the cool sidewalk. I slowly went up to her to rub her stomach to say hello. As soon as

I started to take a few steps away, she was up with her resilient limp and trotting to get ahead of us.

We moved through town streets passing cafés, homes, and various businesses. Her fluffy white tail bounced as she moved. She stopped as we neared the edge of town and began scratching her ear. She watched us the whole time. I couldn't get over how relaxed she was. At this point, I started to get anxious. I first figured she was just supporting us through town but that she would soon be turning back to head home.

Nope.

As we left the quaint streets of town, she turned right and continued moving in front of us. We were all now on a busy high-speed roadway. There were no shoulders. It was stressful enough navigating our own bodies, but I was now panicking over whether or not she would get hit by a car.

Ben was way more relaxed about it. He was like, "It's probably where her limp came from." He smirked and showed no sign of worry. As a dog lover, I was (sort of playfully, but actually) offended and started feeling the need to try to convince her to come our way. Once she was close, I would guide her back to town.

I called for her. I whistled. I clapped. I did the knee-patting dog-talk thing.

Nothing. She wasn't having it.

As cars flew by, my heart kept jumping into my throat. In the meantime, we kept checking the maps and guidebook. The maps were telling us we should be seeing a trail marker sometime soon. The guidebook was helpful but was far from providing easy-to-follow turn-by-turn directions. At least half of the markers we saw, if we saw any at all, were well aged and hard to see.

"Did we miss a turn?

"Do we keep following her?

"I hope we can get off this street soon."

Traffic continued to rush by us in both directions. I frantically flipped through the guidebook while our furry friend continued trotting along. My anxiety increased as we continued trying to find the marker to get off this road. I couldn't help but feel that we were continuing to put ourselves and the sweet dog in danger.

Ben tapped me on the shoulder to look up.

She suddenly took a sharp turn into the road.

She was literally limping and trotting right in front of oncoming traffic.

I was freaking out.

Ben was freaking out.

Cars slammed on their breaks, honked their horns, yelled out the windows, and some swerved on the road. All my fears rushed to the surface. I would be mortified if she was hit. It all happened so fast, and it all felt like slow motion.

We caught up to where she turned into the road. We didn't see her on the street. We didn't see her on the other side. The traffic eventually cleared. There she was. She made it safely across and was just sitting about ten feet from the busy street on a narrow gravel road. She was so calm and content.

We were shocked and grateful.

Once Ben and I crossed the street, she looked at us and looked up toward the new winding road. There were no trail markings or signs anywhere in sight. She assumed we knew to follow her, and she continued to head down the path. Ben and I looked at each other. We looked at the flimsy guidebook.

"Is she literally guiding our path?"

We continued looking at each other. This incredible canine just parted and survived traffic as she limped across a high-speed roadway.

"Is this St Francis?" Ben asked. We laughed, but, really, we wondered.

She was so grounded. Where was our ground? While it was entirely unclear which way was up or where we were headed, we knew that deep down, we had to make a choice. We would either choose to trust our guide or continue slowing her down because we wanted to check the book and "be sure."

We let go.

We started walking up this shady, quiet, rural, narrow gravel path. Her fluffy presence glowed as the sun peeked through the trees. We invited the miracle and magic of it all. She turned right. We followed. She shot up a steep hill; we followed. We saw no markings or signs. We trusted.

We embraced the beauty and mystery of her ways.

We were being guided by the limping, car-parting, Saint Francis wonder dog all along. We came up to a bend four miles from where we started, and before we knew it, she was licking her paws in the shade on Main Street. She didn't need to be thanked. She didn't want to be petted. She knew our purpose, had the time, and showed us the way. Ben and I carried her spirit with us for the rest of our journey and still to this day.

TO BE ASTOUNDED

There is something profound in letting go. There is an entire universe, signaling and guiding us far beyond all the walls, lines, words, and systems we've constructed. What does letting go ask of you? What does it feel like? What does it sound like? There's no need to answer those questions. Be with them. Move with them.

The more I uncover and accept a concept of mystery into my everyday work, relationships, and surroundings, the more alive, spacious, and curious I feel. It leaves me craving to be constantly woven with a magical and mysterious world.

Do you ever gaze into the lines, valleys, and patterns in your hands?

Do you pause to cherish the miracle of an abundant garden?

Do you take the time to hear and feel the cosmos in other living beings?

Can you get lost in the fiery red colors of maple leaves?

Can you accept the brilliance of bright yellow hairs on caterpillars?

Walking as mystery helps us encounter the universe inside us and all around us. With each step or roll, we witness realms that so often don't have words. It asks us to deeply see and be deeply seen. Letting go isn't just walking away; it is walking forward. Into our deeper names. We could all use a good long stroll or roll into the great unknown.

DEDICATED PRACTICE

Take some time to move with the practice below. Do you know the Indigenous tribal lands you are walking or rolling on? Learn from and honor them as you move. Listen to your body. Honor your needs. Honor the lived reality of all who walk or use a wheelchair as their primary form around you. Honor what will work for you, especially depending on your ability, community, and context. No rules. Only invitation.

With the Wind

Grounding: Start by noticing your surroundings. Take them in with a little more intention. Do a full panoramic scan. Look up toward the sky. Look at your hands and feet. Check in with your heart. Notice and honor the ground beneath you. Notice what you lose sight of as you peer farther out. Be present to all the tiny miracles that stand out as you take time to notice. From there, take a couple deep breaths:

As you breathe in, invite acceptance and openness for what is seen and unseen around you.

As you breathe out, allow and invite the wind to help you release plans, ideas, and expectations.

Repeat this a couple more times. Be mindful that as you breathe deeply, you make more room for surprise and mystery alongside your movement.

Prompts: Write the following prompts on separate pieces of paper. Bring them with you and read them to yourself and out loud to accompany your practice. You might pull one at a time at random or have all of them available to you as you move.

- I move with what is seen and unseen around me.
- I move with what is known and unknown inside me.
- I invite my movement to see and nurture all areas of uncertainty in my life.
- I invite my movement to see and acknowledge mystery in all things.
- I am the wind. I am the trees. I am the sunset. I am the spaces between.
- I am the void. I am the stars. I am the universe. I am mysterious and wild.

Movement: As you begin to walk or roll, feel the wind and air as it touches your skin. Notice the unique trees that root and reach around you. Peer out into the unfolding horizon. Observe all that moves toward you, near you, and beyond you. After warming up to your senses and surroundings, begin to seek encounters that make you feel curious. Follow their lead. There is no right or wrong way here. There are no formal directions. There are no plans. There are no routes. There are no destinations.

You and all that is around you is a miracle of moments. Reach out to them. Invite them. Follow the direction of the breeze or the flight of a butterfly. Move toward the sound of calling birds. You might notice large trees in the distance; trust that they might be calling you. Go to them. It is imperative for this practice that you have zero expectations, hard stops, rules, or specific destinations. You are truly moving "with the wind."

Be safe and honor your limitations and needs. Have someone available that you can call to pick you up or check on you if needed.

Timing: The timing is open and free. The only suggestion is to give yourself extra cushion on either end of your protected time so you do not feel rushed in any way.

Location: Go anywhere, everywhere. I highly recommend moving with this practice in a variety of places.

WE MOVE AND WE BREATHE

Here we are. We are still breathing. Our blood is still circulating. The sun is still rising and setting. I am grateful you opened this book and that we could journey together through a sea of imperfect words, worlds, and invitations. I hope you still imagine us moving side by side, as I don't believe there is an end to our connection.

I also hope you visit and revisit these practices, again and again, as we comb the air together.

Into more risking and existing between all our lines, divides, canyons, and dreams.

Into a great sunset calling us to be of a more present, humble, colorful, tender, and courageous way.

Into more unhurried movement with all that is alive in you and all that is alive around you.

ACKNOWLEDGMENTS

If it wasn't for my husband, Ben, and how he supports me and sees me, this book wouldn't be here. I love you forever.

Thank you, Kanoa. My teacher. My mirror. My friend.

Thank you, Mom, Dad, Tracy, Cody, Curtis, Mike, Ann, Carol, Rob, Margaret A., John, Mimi, Russ, Aspen, J.J., Alden, Ram, and all who flow in the fabric of family for loving me for all my years.

Thank you, Intrinsic Paths Patrons, past and current, for seeing me, trusting me, and nourishing my capacity to freely create and write this book. You are my creative wings.

Thank you, Pam, Rev. Dr. Dawn, Monticue, Naveed, Garrett, and Arbolista for contributing your stories to this book. You are gifts to me and I am forever grateful for our friendship.

Thank you, Dawn, Darcy, Nicole, Rachel, Ana, Maria Rosa, Sarah S., Sarah M., Dustin, Chris, Angie, Lindsey, Neenah, Mick, Ian, Sista Otey, Des, Taliah, Teri, Winston, Kim, and every Walk-2Connect cocreator, member, leader, partner, and participant for inspiring a world of companionship and shared vision around the gifts of unhurried human movement and connection.

Thank you to every trail angel, host family, Teri M., Linda & Jim, Chelsa, Howard, Luke, Polly, and the Kiva.org staff for believing in me and supporting our walk across the United States in 2010.

Thank you, Junita, Jose, Shirley, Jenny & Kristy, Lacey, Jolene, Heather, Richard R., Jim & Teresa, Will, Michael P., Randall, Mark B., Christena, Melanie, Ebele, Mollybeth, Nadia, Alicia & John, Steph,

Nicole S., Cole & Kaylanne, April & Marcum, Thom, Richard D., Tina, Janet, Esther, Teresa, Deb, Meg & M.K., Burdock & Heidi, Tara & Greg, Matt, Julie, Jenny K., Kira, Laura & Elsbeth, Jenny G., Cesar, Shane, Kayvan, Phyllis, Lattina, and so many others for how you have touched my heart and nourished my creative journey.

Thank you to every single person I have had the pleasure to move alongside. The aches, laughs, screams, secrets, hardships, dreams, deep breaths, and longings shared between our moving frames live in all these pages.

REFERENCES

Baldwin, James, and Toni Morrison. 1998. *James Baldwin Collected Essays*. New York: Penguin Putnam.

Bonder, Nilton. 2010. *Taking Off Your Shoes: The Abraham Path, a Path to the Other*. Victoria, Canada: Trafford.

brown, adrienne maree. 2017. *Emergent Strategy: Shaping Change, Changing Worlds*. Chico, CA: AK Press.

EMDR Institute. 2020. "History of EMDR." www.emdr.com/history-of-emdr.

Francis, John. 2009. *Planetwalker: 22 Years of Walking, 17 Years of Silence*. Washington, DC: National Geographic Society.

Hanh, Thich Nhat. 2018. *The Art of Living: Peace and Freedom in the Here and Now*. San Francisco: Harper One.

Hanh, Thich Nhat. 2001. *Call Me by My True Names: The Collected Poems of Thich Nhat Hanh*. New York: Penguin Random House.

Jenkins, Peter. 1979. *A Walk Across America*. New York: William Morrow.

Malchik, Antonia. 2020. *A Walking Life: Reclaiming Our Health and Our Freedom One Step at a Time*. New York: Hachette Go.

Mammano, Gina Marie. 2016. *Camino Divina—Walking the Divine Way: A Book of Moving Meditations with Likely and Unlikely Saints*. Woodstock, VT: SkyLight Paths.

O'Mara, Shane. 2019. *In Praise of Walking: A New Scientific Exploration*. London: The Bodley Head.

Roberts, Michael. 2021. "Most Dangerous Streets in Denver." *Westword*. https://www.westword.com/news/denver-most-dangerous-streets-11978490.

Rohr, Richard. 2017. "Daily Meditation." Center for Action and Contemplation. https://cac.org/knowing-through-loving-2017-02-26/.

Rohr, Richard, and Mike Morrell. 2016. *The Divine Dance: The Trinity and Your Transformation*. New Kensington, PA: Whitaker House.

Schmitt, Angie. 2020. *Right of Way: Race, Class, and the Silent Epidemic of Pedestrian Deaths in America.* Washington, DC: Island Press.

Solnit, Rebecca. 2021. *Wanderlust: A History of Walking.* Cambridge, UK: Granta Books.

Speck, Jeff. 2013. *Walkable City: How Downtown Can Save America, One Step at a Time.* New York: North Point Press.

Thurman, Howard. 1980. "The Sound of the Genuine." Commencement address, Spelman College.

Valentine, Ashish. 2020. "'The Wrong Complexion for Protection.' How Race Shaped America's Roadways and Cities." NPR. https://www.npr.org/2020/07/05/887386869/how-transportation-racism-shaped-america.

INDEX

A

Abraham Path, 201
accessibility, 13–15, 44, 62,
    64–66
aching edges, 190–93
Advocating for Our Streets
    (integration practice), 62
Alden. *See* Sagaria-Barritt, Alden
Arbolista, 89
Arkansas River, 105
armor, false, 122–23
Around the Bend and Just Ahead
    (integration practice), 207
art, 162
Atlantic Ocean, 4, 187
automobiles
    considerations for, 65–66
    effects of, 14–15, 63–64
awe, 165–66

B

Baker, Nevada, 203
Baker Beach, 4
Baldwin, James, 76
barefoot, going, 53–54
Barnesville, Ohio, 45
Ben. *See* Purner, Ben
Bland, Sandra, 136
Bonder, Nilton, 51
Boyd, Rekia, 136
Brave Creativity (dedicated
    practice), 166–69

Breathing with Trees (integration
    practice), 90–91
brown, adrienne maree, 32, 91
Brown, Michael, 136
Brumfield, Garrett, 74–75
Bullard, Robert, 72–73
bypassing, grief of, 152–53

C

Camino de Santiago, 171–72, 181,
    200, 208
Camino Divina, 178
Carol. *See* Gifford, Carol
Champion, Lacey, 133
Chimayó pilgrimage, 200–201
Choptank River, 2
Colorado Department of
    Transportation (CDOT), 57, 58,
    60, 61
Colorado River, 161, 199
Connally, Monticue, 92–93
connection
    with Earth, 52–54
    walking as, 32–36
creative wonder, walking as, 159–69
Cruz de Ferro, 181

D

dance, 139
dedicated practices
    Brave Creativity, 166–69
    Felt Knowledge, 77–80

dedicated practices (*continued*)
  Gifts, Naps, and Surprises, 138–40
  How Are We Really Doing?,
    126–28
  I Have What It Takes, 199–201
  individual approach to, 16–17
  Making Waves, 154–56
  Spaces Between, 109–10
  To Know the Ground, 52–54
  Unhurried Witness, 182–84
  Walking as Connection, 32–36
  Who Must I Become?, 96–97
  With the Wind, 212–13
Deep Breathing (integration
    practice), 176
Denver, 19, 57–61, 69, 102, 172
desire lines, 60
Distinct Sounds (integration
    practice), 179–80
Duval, Dawn Riley, 135–37

E

Earth care, walking as, 83–97
ease, inviting, 137–38
EMDR (eye movement and
    desensitization reprocessing),
    26–27
eye contact, 128

F

Felt Knowledge (dedicated practice),
    77–80
Flowing Water (integration
    practice), 175
forest bathing, 90
Fort Collins, Colorado, 195
Francis, John, 23, 177
Funkhouser, Jolene, 203–5

G

gay identity, xii, 8–11, 117–118
Get Wet (integration practice), 134
Gifford, Carol, 102
Gifts, Naps, and Surprises
    (dedicated practice), 138–40

GirlTrek, 27, 69, 70
Great Basin National Park, 203
grief of bypassing, 152–53

H

Hailey. *See* Morgan, Hailey
Hajj pilgrimage, 201
heart wisdom, 94
Heydari, Naveed, 195–99
hiking, 15
Honoring the Night (integration
    practice), 206
How Are We Really Doing?
    (dedicated practice), 126–28
Huguenin, Nicole, 139
human dignity, walking as, 19–36
human right, walking as a, 57–80
humility
  etymology of, 50
  pride and, 51
  walking as, 39–54

I

I Have What It Takes (dedicated
    practice), 199–201
Indigenous peoples, 73, 89, 201
injustice, 13, 44, 65
In Praise of Walking, 26, 163
integration practices
  Advocating for Our Streets, 62
  Around the Bend and Just
    Ahead, 207
  Breathing with Trees, 90–91
  Deep Breathing, 176
  Distinct Sounds, 179–80
  Flowing Water, 175
  Get Wet, 134
  Honoring the Night, 206
  individual approach to, 16–17
  Intention Stones, 181
  Knowing and Unknowing, 50
  A Moving Canvas, 162
  Nature Sees Me, 104
  One-Mile Radius, 67
  Plant Relating, 93–94

Public Restroom Awareness, 44–45
Resistance to Speed, 151
Re-spect and the Second Gaze, 23
Sacred Objects, 121
Safe in Oneself, 24–25
Screams, Howls, and Tears, 192
Shells, Cocoons, and Fallen Branches, 194
Somatic Listening, 107
Spirals and Color, 164–65
Tracing and Nurturing Watersheds, 86–87
Walking Stick, 51–52
Intention Stones (integration practice), 181
Into the Wild, 188
Iraqi refugees, 19–22

J

Jenkins, Peter, 188
Jiner, Pam, 27–28, 69–72
Jolene. *See* Funkhouser, Jolene
justice, 72–73, 150

K

Kailash, Mount, 201
Kanoa (author's dog), 1–4, 39–42, 45–47, 101–102
Kiva Walk Across the USA
duration of, 4
ending point of, 4, 199
experience of, 4–6
first day of, 4–5, 187–90
length of, 199
starting point of, 4
Kiva Walk Lending Team, 6
Knowing and Unknowing (integration practice), 50
Kumano Kodo, 201

L

Lacey. *See* Champion, Lacey
land rights, 85
Lectio Divina (Divine Reading), 182

Letofsky, Polly, 204
Lewes, Delaware, 4
LGBTQIA2S+ identities, xii, 10, 120, 193
listening, somatic, 107
love, unconditional, 30, 118–19, 125

M

Making Waves (dedicated practice), 154–56
Malchik, Antonia, 43, 63
Mammano, Gina, 178
March on Washington, 201
Martin, Trayvon, 136
Martinak State Park, 2
Martinez, Junita and Jose, 86
Matt. *See* Sherman, Matt
McCandless, Chris, 188
meditative movement, 177–79
Meetup, 12
Meg. *See* Sagaria-Barritt, Meg
migration routes, 201
Minho River, 171, 175
MK. *See* Sagaria-Barritt, MK
Moab, Utah, 160
money, effects of, 11
Montbello Walks, 27, 69
Morgan, Hailey, 2–4
Mormon Trail, 201
Moundsville, West Virginia, 39
A Moving Canvas (integration practice), 162
music, 133, 139
mystery, walking as, 203–14

N

naps, 139
nature
connecting with, 52–54, 88–97
Nature Sees Me (integration practice), 104
proximity to, 88–89
separation from, 88, 91
Nhat Hanh, Thich, 24, 105

O

Old Spanish Trail, 201
O'Mara, Shane, 26, 163–64
One-Mile Radius (integration
    practice), 67
Overcome Yours, 74

P

Pacific Ocean, 199
peacemaker identity, 157–58
Pedestrian Dignity, 13–15
pedestrians, 13–15, 27–28, 57–61, 62,
    75, 188–89
People's Ditch, 83–84
personal resistance, 149–50, 154–55
Piediluco, Italy, 208
pilgrim paths, 171–72, 200–201, 208
Pitner, Terri Ann (author's mother),
    113–19
Planetwalker, 23, 177
Plant Relating (integration practice),
    93–94
play, walking as, 131–40
political resistance, 150, 155–56
Pony Express route, 201
Portomarín, Spain, 171
practices. *See* dedicated practices;
    integration practices
presence, walking as, 171–84
pride
    expressing, 143–47
    humility and, 51
Public Restroom Awareness
    (integration practice), 44–45
public transit, 65, 79–80
Pueblo, Colorado, 195
Purner, Ben, 124, 208–11

Q

Quaker City, Ohio, 45
queer identity, xii, 10–11

R

racism, 28, 52, 71, 72–73, 152

relationship
    meaning of, 103
    walking as, 99–110
religion, 45
resistance
    personal, 149–50, 154–55
    political, 150, 155–56
    Resistance to Speed (integration
        practice), 151
    social, 150, 155
    walking as, 143–56
Re-spect and the Second Gaze
    (integration practice), 23
restrooms, public, 44–45
Right of Way, 73
rite of passage, walking as, 187–201
Rohr, Richard, 103, 119–20
Romero Otero, Shirley, 86

S

Sacramento Pass, 203
Sacred Objects (integration
    practice), 121
Safe in Oneself (integration
    practice), 24–25
safety, 58–61, 66
Sagaria-Barritt, Alden, 124
Sagaria-Barritt, Meg, 124
Sagaria-Barritt, MK, 124
Sangre de Cristo Mountains, 85
San Luis, Colorado, 83–84
Santiago de Compostela, 171
Schmitt, Angie, 73
Screams, Howls, and Tears
    (integration practice), 192
self-love, 10–11
Selma to Montgomery civil rights
    route, 201
separation, devastating, 30
Shapiro, Francine, 26–27
shedding, 193–94
Shells, Cocoons, and Fallen Branches
    (integration practice), 194
Sherman, Matt, 159
social resistance, 150, 155

Solnit, Rebecca, 122
Somatic Listening (integration
      practice), 107
Soul 2 Soul Sisters, 135
Spaces Between (dedicated
      practice), 109–10
Speck, Jeff, 63
speed, resistance to, 151
Spirals and Color (integration
      practice), 164–65
The Spot, 172
Stalls, David Milton Cox, 172
Standing Rock, 201
Stanley-Jones, Aiyana, 136
suicide, 6, 8, 48–49, 115
surprises, 138–40, 161–62

T

Thurman, Howard, 124–25, 190
To Know the Ground (dedicated
      practice), 52–54
Tracing and Nurturing
      Watersheds (integration
      practice), 86–87
trail angels, 3
trail networks, 201
Trail of Tears, 201
trees, 89–91

U

Unhurried Witness (dedicated
      practice), 182–84
U.S.-Iraq war, 19–20, 22

V

vestibular system, 43
Via Francigena di San Francesco
      (Way of Saint Francis), 208
Visio Divina (Divine Seeing), 182
vulnerability
      forms of, 119–20
      walking as, 113–28

W

waking up
      challenge of, 17
      effects of, 12
      walking as, 1–17
Walkable City, 63
A Walk Across America, 188
WalkDenver, 70
walking (or rolling)
      as creative wonder, 159–69
      as Earth care, 83–97
      hiking vs., 15
      as human dignity, 19–36
      as a human right, 57–80
      as humility, 39–54
      inclusive meaning of, 15
      as mystery, 203–14
      physical benefits of, 26–27
      as play, 131–40
      as presence, 171–84
      as relationship, 99–110
      as resistance, 143–56
      as rite of passage, 187–201
      safety and, 58–61, 66
      as vulnerability, 113–28
      as waking up, 1–17
Walking as Connection (dedicated
      practice), 32–36
A Walking Life, 43, 63
Walking Stick (integration practice),
      51–52
Walk2Connect, 12–13, 32, 35, 57,
      70, 84
waste, relationship to, 43–44
waterways, 86–87, 95, 134, 175
wheelchairs, inclusive meaning of
      walking and, 15
white supremacy, 29
Who Must I Become? (dedicated
      practice), 96–97
With the Wind (dedicated practice),
      212–13

ABOUT THE AUTHOR

PHOTO CREDIT: DARCY GWEN

JONATHON STALLS (he, his) spent 242 days walking across the United States in 2010 and has continued to walk alongside thousands of people for thousands of miles. He describes himself as a Walking Artist. He advocates and organizes for racial, economic, and social justice, identifies as LGBTQIA2S+ (queer/gay), is currently the creator of Intrinsic Paths and the Pedestrian Dignity campaign, and is the founder of Walk2Connect. Jonathon finished his studies at the Living School for Action and Contemplation in 2017. He has committed much of his life to helping people deepen their relationships to one another, to the natural world, and to themselves at an unhurried pace.

About North Atlantic Books

North Atlantic Books (NAB) is a 501(c)(3) nonprofit publisher committed to a bold exploration of the relationships between mind, body, spirit, culture, and nature. Founded in 1974, NAB aims to nurture a holistic view of the arts, sciences, humanities, and healing. To make a donation or to learn more about our books, authors, events, and newsletter, please visit www.northatlanticbooks.com.